# ALDOUS HUXLEY

*A Biography*

## DANA SAWYER

ALDOUS HUXLEY
*A Biography*

Dana Sawyer

Trillium Press
Maine

Trillium Press Edition  December © 2014

Printed in the United States of America

ISBN-10 0692348247
ISBN-13 9780692348246

Reprint.
Previously published: New York: The Crossroad Publishing Company

*To my daughters, Sophia and Emma*

**Father's Side**                    **Mother's Side**

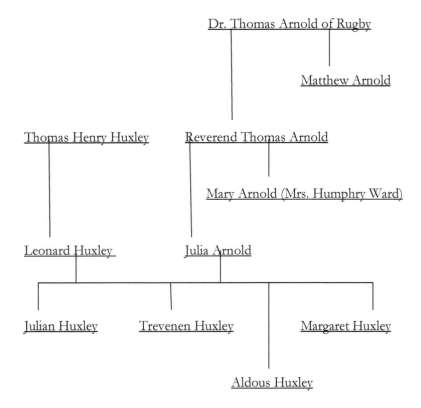

Dr. Thomas Arnold of Rugby

Matthew Arnold

Thomas Henry Huxley        Reverend Thomas Arnold

Mary Arnold (Mrs. Humphry Ward)

Leonard Huxley        Julia Arnold

Julian Huxley        Trevenen Huxley        Margaret Huxley

Aldous Huxley

# CONTENTS

# FOREWORD TO THE SECOND EDITION

When I first wrote this book in 2001, I was motivated to do so for two reasons. First, I was worried that Aldous Huxley was being forgotten, and second, I was struck by the fact that nobody had ever discussed his life in terms of his philosophical ideas. Related to my first concern, that he was being forgotten, I had some confirmation of that when I dropped off the manuscript at the local print shop to make copies for my publisher. When I got ready to leave the shop, the young man waiting on me, who appeared to be about twenty-six, intelligent and articulate, looked down at the cover and said, "I'll have these copies ready for you on Thursday, Mr. Huxley." I had to point out to him that I wasn't Aldous Huxley! It surprised me that he had never heard the name before, given that many of Huxley's books, including *Brave New World,* are still in print.

Regarding the second reason for the book, many scholars have written about Huxley as a literary figure and novelist, and certainly that's appropriate, given that he wrote eleven novels, two collections of short stories and a few books of poetry. However, only eleven of his fifty published works are novels and fewer than twenty of his books can be called 'literature' even in the broadest sense. On the other hand, thirty of his titles deal with philosophical issues of one sort or another, mostly related to moral and social issues, which is why I decided to revisit his life and career. In this book, you'll find his critiques of modern society, his positions on environmental issues, his explorations of Asian religions, and his forays into mysticism, including his experiments with psychedelic drugs. These writings, more than his novels (*Brave New World* and *Island* being exceptions to the rule), still strike me as what make Huxley relevant and keep him our contemporary.

When I agreed to write this book, Crossroad Publishing in New

York commissioned it as part of a series of "spiritual biographies" on such personalities as Frieda Kahlo and Joan of Arc. This got me excited because Huxley had been such a spiritual hero of mine in college. He was intensely critical of organized religion but his study of world mysticism, later published in an anthology titled *The Perennial Philosophy*, had become an inspiration to me, outlining the possibility that people really can wake up out of their robotic slumbers and attain something like the Buddha achieved. When I was young, I found tremendous hope in that prospect, and I still do. Perhaps Huxley was right that the way to create lasting peace in society, and between societies, is by helping individuals to achieve inner peace. That makes sense to me. A forest is only as green as the individual trees in the forest are green, so if we want a peaceful world we need to generate peaceful individuals, and finding one's spiritual center is the key to that. Today, our world is scrubbed clean of the Sacred, but Huxley offers fresh insights for breaking beyond our blinkered view of what we can be, relieving us of the dogmatic materialism in which we've become so deeply mired.

Lastly, I'm glad that this new edition of *Aldous Huxley, A Biography* is coming out when my new biography, *Huston Smith, Wisdomkeeper* (Fons Vitae, 2014), is also available. Huston Smith, the renowned scholar of world religions, was a friend of Huxley's and a student of his ideas. That being the case, I see these biographies as companion volumes, and I'm happy they will be in print at the same time. For more information about these books, or to find out if I'm speaking in your local area, please see my website at dana-sawyer.com. Happy reading! I hope you find the life of Aldous Huxley as engrossing and inspirational as I do.

Dana Sawyer

Portland, Maine
January 6, 2015

# ACKNOWLEDGEMENTS

I first became aware of Aldous Huxley as a college freshman during the Viet Nam war. Introduced to him by a philosophy professor I remember only as "Dr. Rice." I, in my anger and confusion about the war, found strong meaning in Huxley's condemnation of violence between nations. I was drawn to Huxley for his appraisals of blind patriotism and human subjugation to technology but he took me with him on his wild ride through mysticism. Years later, as a graduate student studying Hindu and Buddhist metaphysics, at the Universities of Hawaii, Toronto, and Iowa, I realized I was still sorting out issues Huxley had first put before me in *The Perennial Philosophy*. With reference to questions of ultimate truth and meaning, I find that, like Huxley, I can reach no absolute conclusions—but I thank him for showing me that the search itself is meaningful whether we "arrive" at final answers or not.

My primary sources of information about Huxley's life were the biographies written by Sybille Bedford, Ronald Clark, David King Dunaway, and Laura Archera Huxley, Aldous's widow—who established a charitable foundation, *Children, Our Ultimate Investment*. Beyond these sources I relied heavily on Huxley's own letters, edited by Grover Smith.

For information about Huxley's involvement with the Vedanta Society of Southern California, as well as photographs of Huxley, Isherwood, and Heard, I would like to thank the Vedanta Archives in Hollywood. I am especially indebted to Joanne Euler, who explained to me Swami Prabhavananda's meditation process in long email messages—and then was kind enough to send me tapes and transcripts of Prabhavananda's talks to make sure that I got it right. Likewise, my appreciation goes to the Krishnamurti Foundation of America in Ojai, California, for supplying me with a long transcript of a talk

Krishnamurti once gave on his particular views of meditation.

Of course those who have read all or part of the manuscript for this book and offered their comments and criticisms, must, I certainly hope, know that they have my warmest gratitude. In this regard I particularly wish to thank Art Schliesman, Louise Weiss (my dear friend), Greg Byrer, and Eric Reinders—whose academic expertise in Buddhism provided an important critical dimension. In this regard I am also indebted to Laura Archera Huxley and Dr. Bernfried Nugel, of the Centre for Aldous Huxley Studies at the University of Meunster, Germany, for agreeing to read the manuscript and offer comments. I would also like to thank David Izzo for putting me in touch with Laura Huxley. Additional thanks go to Peter Sarno of PFP Publishing and Annie Wadleigh.

Very special "thank yous" must go to my editor and agent, Barbara Ellis, whose enthusiasm for this project always made me feel like I was onto something; to my philosophy students at the Maine College of Art who were patient with my endless asides about Aldous Huxley; and, most importantly, to my lover and best friend, Stephani Briggs, who read and reread my words, who stayed up so many nights talking with me about Aldous, who fed me while I ranted and researched, and who shows me daily that there is a truth beyond words.

Aldous Huxley in his library, 1956
(Collection of the Los Angeles Public Library)

# - 1 -

# THE NEW REFORMATION

*We live forwards but we can only understand backwards.*

—Soren Kierkegaard

IT WAS THE AUTUMN OF 1960. Aldous Huxley, sixty-six years old and at the height of his intellectual powers, was seated on the stage of the Kresge Auditorium at the Massachusetts Institute of Technology in Cambridge. The hall was packed with an eager audience. Latecomers were sitting in the aisles. Loudspeakers had been placed outside in the corridor, and in two large rehearsal halls where five hundred others—mostly visitors from neighboring Harvard, Radcliffe, Boston University, and Wellesley—waiting to listen. Many more, caught up in the traffic jams Huxley's appearance had set off, never made it in time to hear him.

Huxley, a striking figure with a supremely intelligent face set on top of a six-foot, four-inch frame, said it wouldn't bother him to have people sitting on stage, and so two hundred came up out of the aisles to join him. The Carnegie visiting professor of humanities for 1960—MIT's centenary year—began his lecture, *What a Piece of Work Is Man.* Students and professors alike were quickly drawn into his speech—and into his viewpoint.

Why had they come to hear this man? What was so compelling about him? There were many reasons. Some came simply to see a famous person whose list of close friends and acquaintances read like a *Who's Who* of artists and intellectuals of the twentieth century. But Huxley had had a brilliant career of his own; in fact, he had had

1

three. Aldous Huxley was a novelist and satirist greatly respected by his generation, Sir Isaiah Berlin once comparing him to Ezra Pound as a "great intellectual emancipator." And in what might be called his second career, he wrote about the history of culture and art, an arena in which no less an authority than Sir Kenneth Clark has called Huxley's various analyses the definitive statements on their subjects. But beyond, and perhaps above all this, he became, in his third career, a man of tremendous visionary insight and moral genius.

During the last half of Huxley's life he wrote no less than ten books focusing on the issues that plague humankind. He cast his net broadly, dealing with issues ranging from the impending population and environmental crises (which he talked about before anyone else) to the potentialities of human consciousness and spirituality—leading him even to experiment with LSD. Huxley had become in this last career a philosopher and prophet, and it was in this incarnation that he drew his largest audience. By 1960, through such books as *Ends and Means, The Perennial Philosophy, Adonis and the Alphabet,* and *Brave New World Revisited,* Huxley had become a source of insight and inspiration to tens of thousands.

Though Huxley appears in no academic anthologies of philosophy and held no formal degrees in the subject, he was a philosopher, a "lover of wisdom," in the most important, yet least pretentious, sense of the word. He sought after truth relentlessly—but as a practical man rather than an ivory-tower pedant. Huxley sought not only to understand but to advance—that is, to find what might facilitate our evolution as individuals, as a species, and as a civilization. Huxley believed, as Karl Marx once put it, that "philosophers have only interpreted the world in different ways; the point is to change it."

Huxley was asking hard questions at that time—ones we are still grappling with today. Are we in control of technology? To what extent does technology control us? Will science uncover a truth that provides us with meaning and morality? Or will it continue to erode them both? Can mysticism—and what today is called "New Age" thinking—provide an alternative to scientific thought, or do these constitute simply a regression into superstition and, as Samuel Johnson once said they must, "woolly-mindedness?" "Will the current tendency toward the centralization of political and economic power create Marshall McLuhan's "global village" or will it completely destroy individuality and any real possibility for community? Will we survive the population explosion? Will we live more gently on the earth or continue to move headlong into an environmental crisis? What in our ideology is predisposing us toward these tragedies?

Huxley sought not only to raise these questions but to solve them. This is why so many people came to hear him at MIT that night. They had read Huxley and believed he was onto something.

Reading his books today, we can scarcely disagree. If anything, his views have become more persuasive. And not only because the problems he outlined have become more acute. Huxley was a relentless idea-machine, offering so many practical solutions to such a wide array of problems that even the most jaded and cynical of today's readers still can't help but be drawn into believing that solutions are possible, that there really are intelligent grounds for hope.

Behind and beneath many of Huxley's solutions was a spiritual hypothesis that formed the primary attraction for his audience at MIT in 1960, and continues to form the popular attraction to his work today. Huxley had outlined a position that he believed reconciled science and religion. He proposed the existence of a natural religion—to use his term, a *perennial philosophy*—based on direct experience rather than faith, and the embrace of scientific facts while transcending the technocratic tendency toward materialism. Because his spirituality was a species of mysticism, closely akin to certain schools of Hinduism and Buddhism, it became controversial and many saw in it a compromise of Huxley's genius. But others found in it, and still find, the true flowering of his search for truth and grounds for meaning in their own lives.

No one could do a better job of explaining what Huxley had on his mind than Huxley himself, and to understand his views one has only to read his books. Huxley's journey—encompassing a half-century of inquiry—is a great adventure of the mind, including much of the cultural history of the West for the past two hundred years. And because it centers around the articulation of the issues that we still face today it is also, and to a large extent, our adventure, too.

More than most any twentieth-century figure, Huxley's journey is our own in microcosm.

THE LECTURES HUXLEY GAVE at MIT were refined outcomes of similar visiting professorships he had recently completed at the University of California at Santa Barbara and at the Menninger Foundation in Topeka, Kansas. The lectures were published posthumously as *The Human Situation*. To be a pivotal and influential thinker was quite nearly a birthright for Aldous Huxley. Born into a famous family of British intellectuals who had helped shape the previous century, Huxley began his career as a poet, publishing in 1916 his first book, *The Burning Wheel*. Poetry was a family tradition. Huxley's granduncle, that is, his mother, Julia's, uncle, was Matthew Arnold, the poet, critic and moralist who is considered, along with Tennyson and Browning, one of the greatest Victorian poets.

But important as Matthew Arnold was, and still is, there was another relative of Huxley's, of the same generation as Arnold, who exerted a larger influence on the modern mind—his grandfather, the towering scientist, Thomas Henry Huxley. In some sense it can even be argued that Aldous Huxley was mainly striving to answer questions that his grandfather had forced upon us. For Thomas Huxley was one of the founding figures in the establishment of the Scientific Revolution, a revolution in ideology that many have argued eclipses the Renaissance and the Reformation. Science has become, for better and for worse, the dominant path to truth in Western culture and Aldous's grandfather helped make that so. In part by establishing Darwin's evolutionary theory as an article of faith in the modern mind—a theory that made suspect the divine origin of man and the very existence of God.

Aldous was only one year old when his famous and influential grandfather died, but a man so tall casts a long shadow and Aldous soon became very much aware of who his grandfather was and what had been his place in the world. In fact, when Aldous was only twelve he attended, with his family, the unveiling ceremony for his grandfather's statue, which still stands in the London Museum of

Natural History. The first philosophical worldview that Aldous became aware of was his grandfather's. And many of the philosophical questions he would later wrestle with were direct consequences of theories his grandfather championed, questions his grandfather could not have fully anticipated but nonetheless helped make necessary. In a very real sense, the specifics of Aldous's career and thought were an effect that could be summarized as the sins of the grandfather visited upon the grandson. Thomas Huxley would pull us into the "Space Age," and Aldous Huxley would deal with the consequences.

Aldous's descent from greatness is presented, as his primary biographer, Sybille Bedford, once observed, like a litany. But after the litany is recited it is asked to stand alone, self-evident and unexplained. Certainly that was once possible, but now, more than one hundred years after the death of Thomas Henry Huxley (and that other most important of Aldous's ancestors, Matthew Arnold), and more than a century after the birth of Aldous, some explanation is required. It is not hyperbole to state that Thomas Henry Huxley has had as great an influence on the course of Western civilization as has either Thomas Jefferson or Thomas Edison. As the respected science commentator Loren Eiseley put it in *Darwin's Century,* Thomas Huxley was one of that "little, brilliant band of men who by their united endeavor had swung world thought into a new channel." This new channel became an article of faith in the Huxley family and Aldous began his intellectual journey from that channel, making his grandfather's career worth a short detour.

A name that we remember as part of another great litany that includes Copernicus, Kepler, Galileo, and Newton, is Charles Darwin. It was Darwin's theory of evolution (actually also conceived of independently by Alfred Russell Wallace) that changed, fundamentally, our view of man and his place in the universe. However, Thomas Huxley, more than either Darwin or Wallace, had the crucial role in the establishment of that theory. As one commentator has summarized, "Without Huxley's pugnacious defense . . . the whole basis of evolution for which Darwin provided so much chapter and verse might have remained for decades little more than a scientific curiosity."[1]

When the theory was first presented in 1858, the full import of the Darwin-Wallace discovery was not grasped. In fact, it was given little notice. In part this was because the theory of evolution was not completely new. Jean-Baptiste Lamarck had argued a generation earlier that plants and animals—including humans—had evolved by adjusting to changes in their environments. Consequently, one scientist, Professor Houghton of Dublin, argued that there was little reason to pay attention to the Darwin paper—observing that everything new in it was false and everything true in it was old. But others did not agree, and among these was a brilliant young physiologist, Thomas Henry Huxley. Huxley, who had been admitted to the Royal Society at the age of twenty-five, and who had made his first original scientific discovery at nineteen (of a membrane in the root of the human hair which is still known as the "Huxley layer"), saw that what the Darwin thesis offered was not so much a new theory as a detailed explanation of how the process worked.

Once fully apprised of the Darwin-Wallace theory, Huxley endeavored to prove or disprove it with his own considerable analyses. The result of his study was an overwhelming support for its position and public acknowledgement of that fact. A few years later, in 1863, Huxley published his important book, *Evidence of Man's Place in Nature*, the first treatise to explain in scientific terms what Darwin's theory implied for human origins and our place in the universe. The book came out eight years before Darwin's own treatment of the subject in *The Descent of Man*, but Darwin felt no animosity at having been scooped. Instead, he welcomed the book as eloquent support for his position. Huxley's prose style was more engaging than Darwin's and Darwin himself knew it, once confessing to a friend, "When I read Huxley, I feel quite infantile in intellect."[2]

Huxley knew better than most that Darwin's theory held water scientifically and he, being by nature a pragmatist, became impatient that it should be acknowledged. He urged other scientists to investigate the theory and accept its consequences—whatever they might be—simply because accepting that truth, just as accepting any truth, however difficult, was necessary for a culture to progress. And progress, for Huxley, as for the Victorians in general, was the highest ideal. And why not? Science and technology had created the Industrial Revolution that had made England the richest and most powerful nation in the world. It had precipitated the rise of the middle class, which was quickly growing in size, money, and influence. And Huxley, a member of that middle class, perceived a bright future via science and technology, and so urged his countrymen to accept what he called "the way of the laboratory."

In his writings there are passages in which he doubts that technology only, and necessarily, brings positive benefits, but his tendency was to see any negative consequences—such as the child labor and air pollution of his own time—as the growing pains of a process that is ultimately good and beneficial. That is, he would rather err on the side of over-enthusiasm for science, and clean up any problems or mistakes later, than allow the impetus for progress to be slowed by timidity or allegiance to religious fears. Darwin's theory helped him forward this ideal of science and progress, leading the way toward a true understanding of the world and our place in it, and he embraced it fervently. One consequence of this for the Darwin debate was that Huxley, a brilliant writer and orator, turned what could have been a slow war of attrition into a brilliant campaign.

By 1875 Thomas Huxley had become the most important figure in the British scientific community—taking over science just when science was taking over Victorian civilization. Now secretary of the Royal Society, he had already served as president of the British Association, as well as of the Ethnological and Geological Societies. Though he had less time for research, half the administrative business of English science was carried around in his head. Huxley's success and influence is demonstrated by a trip he made to the United States in 1876, during which he was lauded as a hero of science and in that capacity delivered the inaugural address at the newly constructed Johns Hopkins University.

During the last years of his life Thomas Huxley would find himself increasingly drawn into the wider debate that centered on religious and philosophical questions implicit in evolutionary theory. People were curious about what bright future Huxley could foresee. That is, if our evolution is due to a principle of survival of the fittest, then what exactly is it that we are fit for? The reading public of Victorian England, mostly members of the middle class, were clearly being swayed in the direction that science was leading—but they had questions and worries. When Huxley spoke about what we now call the Scientific Revolution, he told his countrymen, "We are in the midst of a gigantic movement greater than that which preceded and produced the Reformation," and they, with Victorian optimism, hoped he was right. But where was this "gigantic movement" leading? And could science provide a foundation for human meaning and morality? Without the threat of an angry God to punish sinners?

IN 1888 THOMAS HUXLEY, having refused two professorships at Oxford (he believed he could be more effective elsewhere), accepted the prestigious Copley Medal for science from the Royal Society. In that same year, Mrs. Humphry Ward, a popular novelist, published a new book that caused an important stir and popular support for Huxley's position. This collaboration was significant not only to Thomas Huxley's career but also to Aldous Huxley's life, because Mrs. Humphry Ward's sister, Julia, would become Aldous's mother.

Mrs. Ward's novel, *Robert Elsmere*, is the story of a young cleric who becomes a rector in Surrey, England. While living there happily with his young wife and new child he befriends a sinister squire who argues logic and science against the Christian miracles. The eventual result is that Elsmere undergoes a crisis of faith, surrenders his superstition (and his faith along with it), drops his ministry, and moves to London with his family. Once there, rather than wallowing in self-pity, he begins a crusade to feed the hungry, to shelter the homeless, and to help the poor. However, he soon dies of his efforts—a martyr to truth and humanism.

William Gladstone, then prime minister of England, wrote about the novel in the periodical *The Nineteenth Century*, that the novelist had clearly sought to destroy Christianity's "dogmatic structure," while still trying "to keep intact the moral and spiritual results." And Gladstone was right. One consequence of the novel's publication, and the subsequent debate surrounding it, was that a large segment of the population who had never read the *Origin of Species* or any of Huxley's books suddenly became aware of his ideology, summarized in his name for it, "agnosticism." Huxley had invented the term in 1869 after joining a group called The Metaphysical Society. Wishing to consort with proponents of various theological and philosophical positions in order to inform them of a scientific perspective, he joined the group only to realize that everyone but he belonged to some kind of *ism* or another. He was "the only fox without a tail," and so he invented the term agnosticism to signify, a skeptical position with reference to metaphysics. The term quickly became popular.

When the Church Congress of England met in 1888, the year of Mrs. Ward's novel, they discussed agnosticism and came out against the reading of *Robert Elsmere*. The official position of the Congress was published in *The Nineteenth Century* in February of 1889. Readers, including Huxley, learned from Dr. Wace, the principal of Kings College, that the term *agnostic* was only "another word for infidel." Huxley came, necessarily or unnecessarily, to Mrs. Ward's rescue, penning an immediate reply for *The Nineteenth Century*, explaining that agnosticism wasn't anti-Christian or an opposing faith but rather an "open-minded alternative to all dogmatism." Mrs. Ward wrote to agree with him, and soon the duo of Huxley and Ward had done much to establish the agnostic position in the public mind.

*Robert Elsmere* was the high-water mark of Ward's writing career, and so it was unfortunate that a beloved uncle of hers died that same year. Coincidentally, that uncle was also a friend of Thomas Huxley's and he mourned the loss as well. The uncle's name was Matthew Arnold and Mrs. HumphrWeby Ward, born Mary Arnold, was the daughter of Matthew's brother, Thomas Arnold. Her younger sister, Julia Arnold, had married, three years before, in 1885, Thomas Huxley's oldest son, Leonard. And so, Ward's sister was Thomas Huxley's daughter-in-law. Julia Arnold and Leonard Huxley's third son, born in 1894, in a house named Laleham after the village where Matthew Arnold had grown up, was Aldous Huxley.

This was the legacy with which Aldous was raised. Science versus religion was the world into which he was born, and his grandfather and aunt had been principle players in what many called the "New Reformation." Of course, the scientific and technological revolution hasn't had only the positive effects that Thomas Huxley had hoped for. And it has not presented a foundation for meaning and spiritual truth. In fact, in many instances (as Aldous would later point out) it has caused an erosion of meaning and a tendency to perceive values as little more than cultural conventions. It has presented inarguable facts, but it has also left a vacuum. Summarizing this point, Joseph Wood Krutch once observed: "We are disillusioned with the laboratory, not because we have lost faith in the truth of its findings but because we have lost faith in the power of those findings to help us as generally as we had once hoped they might help."[3]

This crisis of faith forms the genesis of Aldous's philosophical and spiritual evolution. He would inherit not only a group of answers and the scientific method that made them possible but also a group of questions. He would begin his mature thought in agreement with his grandfather's position but would quickly extend his own agnosticism to include doubts about any absolutist truth claims—including those of science. He would encourage others also to be skeptical of the way of the laboratory and to recognize its limitations. Thomas Huxley had helped create the Age of Science; and many people in the audience that night at MIT hoped that Aldous could find a way out of it, or at least a humanistic way to temper it. If Thomas had created the twentieth century, they hoped that Aldous might create the twenty-first. The series of lectures that followed that first night at MIT still remains the most popular series in the institution's history.

# - 2 -

# THREE CRISES

*The more science discovers and the more comprehension it gives us
of the mechanisms of existence, the more clearly does
the mystery of existence stand out.*

—Sir Julian Huxley

ALDOUS HUXLEY WAS BORN on July 26, 1894, near Godalming, in Surrey, England. Leonard, Aldous's father, was at that time an assistant master at Charterhouse School and Julia, his mother, was busy raising his two brothers, Julian, age seven, and Trevenen, age five (a sister, Margaret, would be born five years after Aldous). The family, living humbly on a schoolmaster's salary, was by all reports generally happy and glad to be established in the country. Aldous was very close with his brothers, though they called him "Ogie," short for Ogre, because he had an unusually large head, which actually prevented him from walking until the age of two. Trev, the middle brother, once remembered that as a child, "We put father's hat on him and it fitted."

Several family anecdotes and sketches illustrate Aldous's early promise and proclivities. One tells how Aldous, only four, was sitting in a window with a pensive expression when one of his aunts asked, "What are you thinking about Aldous, dear?" He turned from the window and answered, simply, "Skin." Other impressions we have of Aldous as a young boy are that he was friendly but quiet; he fit in but was recognized as different. Julian, the eldest brother, later explained: "From early boyhood I knew in some intuitive way that Aldous possessed some innate superiority and moved on a different level from us other children." This certainly constitutes high praise, since Julian himself would later become a world-renowned scientist and author, knighted by the queen.

Leonard Huxley, the eldest of Thomas Huxley's sons, had attended Balliol College at Oxford and had studied law. He was remembered as a good-looking, athletic (especially fond of ice skating and mountaineering), hardworking, and popular young man. He was not a genius, but his gifts were far from meager. Later in his life he would write several commendable and popular books (including the definitive biography of his famous father), and edit several others, most notably the letters of Elizabeth Barrett Browning. He had been pushed to study law by his father, and also by the master of Balliol, a family friend. However, Leonard never became a barrister, for he had met at Oxford a young woman, Julia Frances Arnold, whom he wished more fervently to marry than studying law would allow.

Julia Arnold was a bright and attractive young woman, at the time finishing her own education at Somerville College at Oxford (receiving, in 1882, a degree in English with first honors). How much the fame and position of their respective families influenced Leonard and Julia's eagerness to marry is difficult to gauge, but such motivations were common in Victorian England and had a different cultural import than they would today. Whatever the degree of motivation from that source, Leonard chose, against the wishes of his father, a career in teaching as a shortcut to the financial means necessary for the couple to wed.

As has often been pointed out, Leonard and Julia's marriage was much more than the marriage of two people; it was the marriage of two great families, the Arnolds and the Huxleys. Aldous Huxley was the product of two prestigious branches of a class within a class— that is, the governing upper middle class—who, though not of the "noble blood," nonetheless constituted the intellectual aristocracy of the British Empire.

In the late nineteenth century the middle class in England was only one fifth of the total population, and the elite of that class into which Aldous was born, was made up of only a few families—the

Arnolds and Huxleys among the most prominent. Being born at that time and in that place was fundamental to the development of Huxley's mind, for his inherited culture and its requisite obligations of class were to influence him all his life. Although he modified and refined his personal philosophy continuously, his basic disposition toward philosophy itself never changed. He believed that ideas, ultimately, have no inherent value—that in order to be good they must not only be true but useful. This was part of his Victorian inheritance. The Victorians believed that progress was possible and desirable, but each person, according to his ability, must do his share to make it happen. The British Empire was at the height of its power and influence in the late nineteenth century but the middle class hoped to steer it in an even more progressive direction.

When the Industrial Revolution had caused the middle class to emerge, moralists among them such as Carlyle and Ruskin, basing their thoughts on eighteenth-century Enlightenment perspectives, impressed upon their followers that they must be wary not to recreate feudal despotism. A new economic and political order had allowed them to rise above peasantry, and they must not become insensitive to the suffering of those whom the new order hadn't yet lifted up. Joining charitable organizations and working for the welfare of the poor was considered a moral obligation by most. Those who were "better off" should be of service, not for the poor's sake but for their own moral advancement—to fulfill their responsibility to society. Though this philanthropy was sometimes embraced dispassionately and out of a sense of obligation, it was nonetheless a widespread ideal of the middle class—and especially in the upper middle class. The most remembered example and embodiment of this moral imperative is, of course, Florence Nightingale, who, from an affluent family, devoted herself to nursing the poor and unfortunate.

Among intellectual families, such. as the Huxleys, Arnolds, and Darwins, this calling to benefit society was specifically conceived as a project of the mind—for the mind was their particular domain. These families believed they could best serve their nation by extending the limits of knowledge, by cultivating aesthetic sensibilities, and by searching for truth. Though Aldous would eventually arrive at a different worldview than his grandfather's, both he and Thomas Huxley shared their class's characteristic passion for knowledge as public service.

One consequence of the intellectual families' position in society, and their perception of themselves as the caretakers of truth and culture, was that they could be intimidating to meet and were sometimes overly snobbish. Some writers have blamed this on the customs of the time, including the tendency of the middle class to adopt not only the tastes but also the superficial mannerisms of the aristocracy—as a way of distancing themselves from the lower classes (including, in many cases, the classes from which their families had come). But regardless of its origins, snobbishness is today considered one of the defining characteristics of the Victorian upper middle class, and Aldous himself could at times be guilty of sticking his nose in the air—which, since he was exceedingly tall, placed it very high indeed.

Another consequence of the intelligentsia's obligation to forward knowledge and truth was the tendency to put enormous pressure on their children to learn and perform well in school. Living up to one's potential was not only a responsibility to oneself but a responsibility to one's society. One must let one's light shine as a means of supporting the common good. Examples abound of Victorian children who were driven to enormous success—or nervous breakdown—by parents intent on their living up to their potential.

In addition to the obligations imposed by culture and class, Leonard and Julia Huxley's three sons had also to bear the obligation of being from a prestigious family, in fact, from two prestigious families. This was a pressure of some proportion, as testimonies from several of Aldous's cousins make clear. Roger Eckersley, another grandson of Thomas Huxley, once wrote: "The Huxley connection has always been an embarrassment to me as I was always expected to be so much cleverer than I was."[1]

Aldous became aware of these responsibilities to class and family at an early age and mostly from his mother. Julia Arnold had not only attended Oxford but she had grown up there. She was very cultured, in the Victorian manner, and was used to having interesting people around her. (She was one of a group of children often photographed by Lewis Carroll, who later wrote *Sylvie and Bruno* for Julia and her

Matthew Arnold, circa 1851, above, and below,
Thomas Henry Huxley, "Darwin's bull dog," circa 1857

(National Archive, Washington, D.C.)

Thomas Henry Huxley and his
grandson, Julian Huxley

(National Archive, Washington, D.C.)

two sisters.) Julia knew her obligations and saw it as a moral duty to pass them on to her sons. Leonard, on the other hand, though in agreement with this position, was not as focused on his children or as disciplined as Julia. So it was left to Julia to become the shaping force and guiding light.

Julia Huxley—slim, pretty (in a rather prim way), and very bright—was also, and at once, disciplined and nurturing. Aldous, her youngest son, was devoted to her, once writing, in a thinly disguised portrait, that she had a "transcendent honesty" and that "you felt the active radiance of her goodness when you were near her."

As Julia's boys grew she expected great things from them, and threw herself into their development with a will. She would give them the best chances and the best schools. This would be one way she could fulfill her obligations to class and family, but (as promising as her boys looked) it wouldn't be the only way. In 1902 she opened Prior's Field, a school for girls. (Aldous, however, at age eight, while his parents were trying to decide where to place him, did attend one term at Prior's Field.) Julia continued to urge her sons to live up to their obligations. "Huxleys always get firsts" (first honors) became the family motto. Though this certainly imposed considerable pressure to succeed, Aldous seems to have accepted it well. At times, and especially when young, he felt the pressure but thought that studying hard actually suited him. He was a natural scholar and later remarked, "As it happens, I have the kind of mind to which an academic training is thoroughly acceptable. Congenitally an intellectual, with a taste for ideas and an aversion from practical activities, I was always quite at home among the academic shades. Liberal education was designed for minds like mine."

PRIOR'S FIELD GREW QUICKLY—moving from six girls to fifty in just two years—and the school is still open today. Julia's success with the school was likely helped by the Arnold-Huxley aura but accounts make it clear that she was also competent in running it. Julia had grown up in a family of educators and understood the discipline of teaching very well. Her grandfather had been Dr. Thomas Arnold, the famous reformer and headmaster of Rugby School, and Matthew

Arnold, her uncle, though remembered as a poet, was in fact an inspector of schools for thirty-five years and took his job quite seriously. How seriously is indicated by the fact that when he eventually was offered, and accepted, a position teaching poetry at Oxford, he did not quit his job as inspector of schools.

Arnold's views on education and its supreme necessity for advancing culture greatly influenced his niece and, through her, his grandnephew, Aldous. In fact, Matthew Arnold's views became as important to the direction of Aldous Huxley's thinking as did Thomas Huxley's, forming the other half of his intellectual launch-pad. Arnold's reticence about "the way of the laboratory" was as much a part of Aldous Huxley's thinking as was Thomas Huxley's enthusiasm for it, and the former would temper the latter and contend with it all his life.

Arnold worried that as the middle class emerged and gained more leisure and opportunity it would squander both on vacuous entertainments. He worried that the quality of art and literature would plummet as the market for such commodities became influenced by the bourgeois tastes of the buying public. And he worried that the growing tendency of the Victorian middle classes to embrace Puritanism as a foundation for morality would lead his culture in the wrong direction, himself believing that Puritanism was "too narrow and inadequate" a vision ever to "bring humanity to its true goal." Arnold argued that people must work to become open-minded and curious, and that they should refuse to take things on authority without thinking for themselves. Consequently, Puritanism—and the religious dogma that went with it—was not the proper path because it cultivated "strictness of conscience rather than spontaneity of consciousness."

Arnold worried, prophetically, that the future would belong to the middle classes but that they would be ill equipped to meet the challenge. Remembered today as a great Victorian poet, he was also a great Victorian moralist—though he disagreed with Carlyle and Ruskin on a fundamental point. Where Carlyle and Ruskin argued that the middle classes were a scourge because they were materialistic and selfishly indifferent to the poor, Arnold contended that they were actually more ignorant than wicked. They were only "Philistines" because they lacked proper education. He argued this point repeatedly in public lectures as well as in books such as *Culture and Anarchy*.[2]

ONE OF ARNOLD'S PRINCIPLE allies in the fight for better and more widespread education was Aldous's grandfather, Thomas Huxley. Like Arnold, he was worried about the Philistines and Puritans and he liked Arnold's arguments against both, sometimes borrowing from them to use in his own lectures. One result of their common cause was that the two men began a correspondence and a friendship.

However, there was one point upon which they deeply disagreed, and that was Huxley's belief in the supreme importance of scientific education. Arnold, as an intellectual, was not opposed to scientific thought but he gave it less weight than Huxley. It was true that science and technology had brought much that was good into the world but they hadn't brought only good. They also had increased the pace of life and the pace of change to breakneck speed. Not only that, industrialization had brought such physical maladies as air pollution and child labor. But above and beyond this, there were ideological ramifications that must be faced. Science was profoundly, and often adversely, affecting people's views of their world and their place in it.

Arnold was aware that science had not only undermined the traditional physical view but also the traditional philosophical view of the world. Even if one believed, as many intellectuals did, that the facts of science couldn't be denied, what would be the ideological consequences of embracing them? Fears about the possibilities— even before Darwin—had lead Tennyson, Arnold's contemporary and friend, to call geology and astronomy the new "terrible muses" of literature because they had changed Western culture's conception of nature in the direction of a cold and uncaring machine. In Arnold's own case, he worried that as science eroded the traditional foundations of morality and meaning, it would not, as Huxley argued, bring with it an implicit new structure of morality and meaning to fill the void.

In 1851, while the popular culture celebrated the Crystal Palace and the London Exposition advertised British technological know-how, Arnold wrote his most famous poem, *Dover Beach*. In the poem, Arnold says that he hears the ebb of the "Sea of Faith" moving away with "its melancholy, long, withdrawing roar." And here he reveals himself as a modern voice, for though it was Thomas Huxley's science and scientific worldview that would eventually win the day, it is Matthew Arnold's alienation and despair more than Huxley's optimism that have come to characterize the modern mind. When Arnold writes in *Dover Beach* that "we are here on a darkling plain," he is clearly anticipating the loss of meaning presented in Eliot's *The Wasteland,* the severe landscapes of Camus's existentialism, and the moral limbos of Aldous Huxley's early novels.

Arnold was an artist and esthete; he stressed inwardness and self-knowledge as the foundation of truth and culture, whereas Thomas Huxley stressed outwardness, utility and knowledge of the world. Huxley felt that widespread scientific education would allow the best and brightest, of whatever class, to come forward and have their powerful and necessary influence on society. But Arnold feared that that influence would be within too narrow and materialistic a range of concern. In his 1883 essay "Literature and Science," he tells us that scientists see the world too mono-dimensionally, overlooking the human sense of conduct and its sense of beauty. "Men," he tells us, "cannot live by formulas alone," and he returns to an argument he had been making for years (one that Aldous would later borrow and play upon all his life): that man is a creature of many sides and dimensions, and that people must therefore cultivate all their possibilities—artistic, spiritual, and physical. "A human nature complete on all its sides, remains the true ideal of perfection still," he writes in *Culture and Anarchy*, advocating that curricula be broadened. But Arnold's inwardness smacked of romanticism to Thomas Huxley and he held a hard line for more science.

The disagreement between Huxley and Arnold, and the issues that it raised, not only formed the intellectual environment into which Aldous was born but also provided the central issues he would revisit all his life. Aldous would become a rationalist, but he worried about the fetishization of science, the tendency to worship it without reflection or acknowledgment of its limitations. Like Arnold, he wanted to educate and uplift the whole man, not just his rational function, and, and, also like Arnold, he saw himself as a gadfly to the status quo and the narrow-minded. Both men began their careers as poets but found their true calling writing essays to enlighten the masses.

IN 1903, WHEN ALDOUS WAS NINE, he entered the "academic shades" humbly, starting his education at the nearby Hillside School, which he would attend until he was fourteen. Leaving Hillside in the fall of 1908 he followed his brothers to Eton—though they had already graduated and were then studying at Balliol. The program at Eton focused on the classics, Tuesdays being entirely devoted to composing Latin verses. Aldous was good at the classics, especially Greek, and held a King's Scholarship. First year students at Eton were called "fags," and fags were required to do most of the menial chores around the school (setting the tables, lugging the bath water, etc). Aldous, like the other boys, wasn't fond of "fagging" but bore it well and later had good memories of his time at Eton. One classmate later described him as a "tall, lanky youth with a thick shock of hair"; he was only fourteen but already near his adult height.

Aldous's life had been idyllic up to this point. He had grown up in the country, had attended the best schools, and had spent several summer vacations with his family in Switzerland. However, in November he experienced the first of three shocks to his young life. These three life crises are important because they pushed him toward an early pessimism that colored his first mature outlook.

First, and after only a short period of illness, his mother, Julia, died of cancer at the age of forty-five. He hadn't really known what was happening with his mother until he was called home from school to see her for the last time. Aldous, who was often autobiographical in his novels, gave an account of that last visit, expressing not only his grief but also the poignancy of Julia's last lesson to her youngest son, in his second novel, *Antic Hay*. "He hadn't known that she was going to die, but when he entered her room, when he saw her lying so weakly in the bed, he had suddenly begun to cry, uncontrollably. All the fortitude, the laughter even, had been hers. And she had spoken to him. A few words only, but they had contained all the wisdom he needed to live by. She had told him what he was, and what he should try to be, and how to be it. And crying, still crying, he had promised that he would try." Given his love for his mother and the obligations she instilled in him, the importance of this promise is difficult to overemphasize.

Aldous bore his grief with courage; however, in his 1941 book *Grey Eminence*, he summarizes the effect of his mother's death on his later life in the context of explaining Francois Leclerc du Tremblay's feelings for the loss of his father at the age of ten. "There remained with him, latent at ordinary times but always ready to come to the surface, a haunting sense of the vanity, the transience, the hopeless precariousness of all merely human happiness." In Huxley's later explorations of Hinduism and Buddhism he would find ideological support for this personal sentiment.

During the next three years Aldous was busy with an education that was increasingly leading him in the direction of science. He wished to become useful to society by becoming a doctor and specializing in medical research. That was not to be though, for in the next year he suffered his second crisis. Early in the winter of 1911 he began having problems with his eyes. Time passed but the illness remained. It worsened to the point that Aldous had to leave Eton, turning up at his aunt, Ethel Collier's, house with a case of "pinkeye." Rest did not help the condition and Aldous continued to lose his eyesight. The eventual diagnosis was *keratitis punctata*, an inflammation of the corneas, which made him virtually blind for eighteen months. The cause of the trouble has never been clearly determined. There were rumors of a lab accident at Eton, which Aldous never confirmed; his cousin Gervas Huxley speculated that Aldous had gotten "infected dust" in his eyes while suffering from a bout of flu.

Seeming destined for a life of blindness, Aldous got on with his life stoically and as best he could. He lived with various relatives, including the Henry Huxleys (Gervas's parents), the Humphry Wards, and the Selwyns, who were watching after his younger sister, Margaret. Leonard Huxley was by that time living in London. He had taught at Charterhouse for fifteen years but became dissatisfied when there were no prospects for advancement. Then, in 1900, a new possibility had presented itself. He was offered the job of writing his father's biography and did so to critical acclaim. One success led to another and Mrs. Humphry Ward, Julia's sister, got her publisher to offer Leonard, on the strength of his recent book, a position as a reader and literary advisor. The job included a partial editorship of *The Cornhill*, a well-known literary magazine. Leonard liked the work and thrived in his new job, which eventually took him to London where he was living a bachelor's life at the time Aldous contracted his eye problem.

Aldous, away from his classmates, had a great deal of spare time and taught himself Braille, using it to learn to play the piano. Lewis Gielgud, a close friend from his Hillside school days, and the elder brother of Sir John Gielgud, the actor, also taught himself Braille, so they could keep up a correspondence. Trev also gave special attention to his brother Aldous during this period. Trevenen, who's been described as "agonizingly sensitive, chiefly for others," had been appalled at Aldous's blindness and stepped in to provide support, much as he had done for Aldous and Margaret when their mother had died. In fact, Margaret once claimed that after their mother's death Trev had become the "hub of the family wheel."

One positive and accidental by-product of Aldous's illness was that the intense pressure to excel and hold up the Huxley record was now let up. He had become free to study and think as he willed. Clearly, his future as a doctor was no longer possible. He would have to find 'something else to do. But what? While that was stewing, Aldous spent his time reading in Braille whatever his mind fancied, including the classics and a rich sampling of French literature, old and new. He even wrote an eighty-thousand-word novel that unfortunately was lost, and he became deeply interested in music, crediting the loss of his eyesight with a new acuity of hearing. He later also credited his condition with the development of his legendary memory for facts and details—a memory that would serve him well later in his cross-discipline explorations of all subjects imaginable.

After eighteen months and four operations Aldous's eyes began to clear a bit; one of them, the left eye, improving to about seventy percent of its original capacity, so that he could read with a large magnifying glass. The inflammation had long since subsided, but it left opacities in the corneas that seriously compromised his ability to see. This affliction caused Aldous throughout his life to explore cures, conventional and unconventional, for poor eyesight, and later he would write a book, *The Art of Seeing*, based on his experiments with one specific method.[3]

In the spring of 1912 Aldous went to live in London with his father for a few months. Leonard, now age fifty-two, had remarried that February to Rosalind Bruce, a woman thirty years his junior. Trev, who was in fact a bit older than Bruce, was the only one of Leonard's children to immediately welcome her to the family. Aldous was appreciative of her help in taking care of him while he was at his father's in London, and in later years be would grow to be fond of her. She would give him two half brothers, one of whom, Andrew, would win the Nobel Prize for physiology in 1963, keeping up his own end of the Huxley name.

At the beginning of the new year of 1913, Aldous made plans to prepare for entrance into Balliol. He and Trev had worked it out that they would live together and Trev would help him study and go through the application process. During the following spring and early summer they were inseparable, and Aldous's chances of matriculation were very promising. Trev was twenty-three and in his last term at Balliol but still enjoyed having his eighteen-year-old brother around. They spent their afternoons walking, punting on the river, visiting friends, and reading. Trev was well-liked and regarded as the most personable and accessible of the three Huxley brothers.

In July Aldous spent two months in Grenoble, France, working on his French (which was becoming very good), and that October he started college. He had to keep the pupil of his better eye dilated with atropine so that he could see around the opacity in it to read, but he read voluminously, and used his studies and wit to quickly become a favorite among his peers. Raymond Mortimer, a fellow freshman at Balliol that term, later remarked that he was "formidably sophisticated," "dazzling," and "had read everything."

This was Oxford before the wars, in fact before cars, and Aldous's college room overlooked one of the busiest streets in town. Gervas Huxley described the room as having a piano—upon which Aldous introduced his friends to jazz—and a large French poster of bare-breasted girls at the beach. "The room seemed always full of people talking and laughing. . . It was the centre where the elite of the year gathered . . . . We took all that Oxford had to offer. And it was an awful lot."[4] But that year of fun and glory ended in the summer of 1914.

IN AUGUST ALDOUS WAS IN SCOTLAND with his father, his stepmother, and his brother Julian—now a scientist and home on vacation from a new teaching post in Texas. Trev could not be with them as he had recently become ill with a severe depression. Several pressures had contributed to his condition. He had scored a "second" on his final exams at Oxford the previous spring, and more recently, he had performed poorly on a civil service exam. In his own eyes, he had let down the Huxley name. To make matters worse, it is likely that his performance on these tests was adversely affected by worries he was having about a love affair. The affair involved a girl whom it was impossible, in the social circumstances of that time, for him to marry—at least, not without causing them both much unhappiness. The pressure of these worries had combined to cause a nervous breakdown and on psychiatric advice he entered a nursing home to rest.

News reached the family in Scotland one day that Trev, who had lately seemed on the upswing, was missing from the nursing home. Since he was getting better, the family tried not to worry or think the worst. However, a few days later, the news reached them that Trev's body had been found in the woods. He had hanged himself at the age of twenty-four. This was a jolting tragedy for the entire family but perhaps more so for Aldous who had been recently so close to his brother.

Aldous's father later attributed Trev's death to "exhaustion, worry, and overwork," but Aldous attributed it to his conscience. "It is just the highest and best in Trev—his ideals—which have driven him to his death . . . "[5] Aldous knew that Trev believed he had let down the family and that he had compromised the virtue of a woman he loved. Compromising those ideals had been more than he could bear. Tragedies such as Trevenen's were not rare and serve to illustrate the pressures under which the Victorians and the Georgians of the upper classes were raised.

Aldous had just turned twenty and had already lost the two family members he was closest to, in addition to most of his eyesight. Years later he would confess to his future sister-in-law, Juliette (Julian's wife), that the cynicism of his early novels owed a lot to the disillusionment he felt from those early catastrophes. Today Aldous Huxley is generally thought of as a guarded optimist, an author whose viewpoint is edifying even when (and sometimes because) it is critical of modern culture. But this is only the tone of his later work. Before he found that particular vision and voice he would begin his spiritual search in a dark place, on Matthew Arnold's "darkling plain," and with the First World War about to begin, others would soon be joining him. However, during Aldous's most cynical phase (about to begin) he also formed several friendships that became shaping influences on his life and work, including those with TS. Eliot, D.H. Lawrence, and his future wife, Maria Nys.

# - 3 -

# GARSINGTON

*'To discover one's spiritual poverty is to achieve*
*a positive conquest by the spirit.*
—William Barrett

IN OCTOBER OF 1914 HUXLEY, just twenty, was back at Oxford to continue his studies. Balliol was not the same that fall. He missed his brother terribly, writing to a family friend: "Oh God, it's bitter sometimes to sit in this room reading before the fire—alone and to think of all the happy evenings we sat there together and all the hours I hoped to have again, when he was better."[1] It was also a bitter fall because that August, the same month that Trev died, England had declared war on Germany. Aldous was again abandoned as thousands of young men enlisted in the military, including his two allies from childhood, Lewis Gielgud and his cousin, Gervas. Aldous, also eager to serve, was declared unfit even for noncombat positions by the recruiting board because of his eyes.

Though life was continuing to be difficult for Huxley in 1914, his luck would soon change. In fact, within eight years he would be the most prominent young novelist in England, admired by his contemporaries and, though not yet thirty, discussed by critics in the same breath as Virginia Woolf and James Joyce. But that time was still to come.

He was, and had been, a voracious reader and kept this up in his second year at university. However, the primary course of study for those majoring in English was Anglo-Saxon literature which lent "backbone" to the curriculum (as he complained in a letter to his old headmaster from Hillside) but which Aldous found exceedingly boring. Huxley, though, was too inquisitive simply to be mired in boredom, and he read other things instead. At the center of his self-directed studies was his continued fascination for French literature—endemic to the times (as Alexander Henderson has pointed out: Just before the First World War, .. "The important things in English literary life were mostly French."[2]). He read Proust's *Du Cote de chez Swann* when it came out that year and plunged into the French symbolist poets, mostly Mallarme and Rimbaud. He even modeled some of his own poems on Mallarme's style and—two years later—would publish the first English translation of Mallarme's "The Afternoon of the Faun" in *Oxford Poetry*.

Huxley had decided to be a poet, and in typical Huxley fashion he worked at it diligently. Before he was twenty-six he would produce four volumes of poems: *The Burning Wheel, Jonah, The Defeat of Youth,* and *Leda*. Although poetry eventually ceased to be his focus, critics took his verses seriously and he was generally considered promising. In the period between 1917 and 1921 he was often asked to read in public, sometimes in company with his close friend of the time, T.S. Eliot. Huxley even shows up later as a character in Katherine Mansfield's story *Bliss*, as "a young man, Eddie Warren, who had just published a little book of poems and whom everybody was asking to dine."

Huxley, still struggling with his eyesight, managed to get through his first year back at college after the loss of Trev. The Haldanes, a family who lived in north Oxford, who had befriended Aldous through their daughter Naomi, realized he had been left behind and, given the challenges of his poor eyesight, had asked Aldous to move in with them, which he did. The Haldanes gave him wonderful support, and he had his fascination for French poetry to keep him occupied. But the next year, in 1915, during his third and last year at Oxford, Aldous would do much more than simply get by. He would undergo a tremendous growth spurt in his development as an intellectual and artist. And this would result, directly, from visits he made to a country estate eight miles south of Oxford called Garsington

Manor.

In December, its owners Philip Morrell, a Liberal member of Parliament, and his wife, Lady Ottoline, invited the young Huxley to lunch. Exactly what first drew Huxley to the Morrells, and vice versa, isn't completely clear. Aldous had been recently rethinking his position on the war ("One anticipates," he wrote his father, "that none of one's friends will be left alive. A bloody waste . . ."), and Philip Morrell was one of the few political figures who spoke out openly against the war. His wife, Lady Ottoline, the daughter of a duke, was a well-known patron of the arts, who always had an eye for new talent. Huxley may have been hoping for support, and Ottoline couldn't help but be impressed with Aldous. As Cyril Connolly, the writer and critic, observed years later: "Witty, serious, observant, well-read, sensitive, intelligent, there can have been few young writers as gifted as Huxley."[3]

Whatever the initial attraction on Huxley's part, his first review of the Morrells and their "lovely Elizabethan manor" was mixed. "Lady Ottoline," Aldous wrote his father, "Philip's wife, is a quite incredible creature—arty beyond the dreams of avarice and a patroness of literature and the modernities. She is intelligent, but her affectation is overwhelming. Her husband, the MP, is a conceited ass, very amiable, but quite a buffoon." Within three months though his assessment had improved considerably and he wrote to Julian: "The Morrell household is among the most delightful I know: always interesting people there and very good talk: I go over from Oxford often to see them."

During that last year at Oxford, Huxley was not only figuring out what he wanted to be, he was also working closely on knowing who he was. Certainly he had inherited many convictions from his family, but who was he aside from those convictions? Garsington helped him to find out.

Today Garsington is famous (then it was infamous) as a gathering place for some of the most influential writers and intellectuals of the twentieth century. They were uniformly opposed to the war (which gave Garsington the reputation in town of being a hotbed of German spies) and they were exploring new directions in art and literature. Regular visitors to Garsington during the two years that Aldous was often there included Virginia Woolf, T.S. Eliot, D.H. Lawrence, and Katherine Mansfield. And novelists and poets weren't the only guests of the Morrells. Others included Lytton Strachey, the biographer, who in 1918, created a tremendous stir with his book *Eminent Victorians*, a critical appraisal that is often cited as the highwater mark of anti-Victorian sentiment; Roger Fry, who taught Aldous much about art and art history; John Middleton Murry, the editor who later became Huxley's boss at the *Athenaeum*; Clive Bell, the critic, who was married to Woolf's sister, Vanessa; and, last but not least, the philosopher Bertrand Russell, who was then living at Garsington. Russell had been teaching at Cambridge before the war and was already famous for his publication of the *Principia Mathematica*; however, he was at Garsington doing farm labor to fulfill his alternate service as a conscientious objector. Russell's presence contributed to rumors that Garsington was not only for spies but also for cowards and shirkers.

What was actually going on at Garsington was a continual ad hoc conference on all things intellectual and artistic. Lady Ottoline took her salon seriously and worked to create a forum for people whose work she admired and whom she felt had promise. Into the former category fit the established artists such as Woolf and Mansfield, and into the latter, the comers-up, like Eliot and the very young Huxley.

The company must have been somewhat intimidating for such a young person, but reports suggest that Aldous held his own. He was certainly bright and sophisticated, not to mention a striking figure: "a most singular speckly-eyed young man," Virginia Woolf observed after their first meeting. He was also a bit of a dandy in those days, and for a time even took to wearing a monocle. In a letter to Julian he poked fun at himself, remarking, "My monocle is very grandiose, but gives me rather a Greco-Roman air of rococity." Leonard Woolf, a publisher and the husband of Virginia Woolf, later remarked that Aldous was always "immutably himself among the vast, heterogeneous collection of human exhibits."[4]

But to say that he was not overwhelmed is not to suggest that he was not influenced. He was—and not only with regard to the war.

Europe was changing, rapidly and dramatically, and physically and ideologically, and this was having a landmark influence on the direction of the arts. The crowd at Garsington was well aware of these changes in European culture, and they were developing new ideas and art forms to reflect them—branches of what is today called modernism. This was Huxley's first mature viewpoint and the spark behind his early novels.

THE EARLY VICTORIANS didn't know what human perfection would look like (though the Crystal Palace built for the London Exposition of 1851 pointed a direction) but they were certain it was possible. In the second half of the nineteenth century popular enthusiasm for science was at its apogee, and, for the most part, this would continue to be true until the First World War. This was a period that essayist Joseph Wood Krutch later called the "Age of Confidence." To a large extent, this mass appeal was driven by the array of recent inventions. In the fifteen years prior to Aldous Huxley's birth the world had seen the telephone (1879), the combustion engine (1886), and the light bulb (1888)—and two years after his birth, the radio (1896). He came into the world at the same time as the Eiffel Tower, then the world's tallest structure and a symbol of confidence in science and technology.

But beyond these developments people had also come to believe in science ideologically, as Thomas Huxley had hoped they would, perceiving it as more than just a method for developing tools and comforts but also as a means for finding truth and value. Consequently, enthusiasm for the "way of the laboratory" transcended the traditional scientific disciplines (geology, chemistry, biology, and physics) and was applied to issues of human meaning. In the last half of the nineteenth century the Western world had witnessed the growth of the humanistic sciences: psychology, sociology, comparative religion, anthropology, etc.

The ideology based on this enthusiasm was called *positivism*. The term was coined by Auguste Comte, in his work, *The System of Positive Philosophy* (published in six volumes between 1830 and 1842). Comte, today considered the father of modern sociology, argued that there "are just as definite laws for the development of the human race as there are for the fall of a stone." Comte held that once he had discerned those laws he could use them to direct social and cultural progress. They could be used to correct our appraisal of history (so that we could find out what had *really* gone on), or, more importantly, they could be used to reorganize society along rationalist lines. Comte's enterprise was exactly the kind of direction for which Thomas Huxley had hoped. For centuries the Church had told the human race what it should be but now it could, and would, find out for itself.

Comte and other positivists uncovered many basic facts but, disconcertingly, very little headway was made in uncovering a scientific bedrock for morality or a higher purpose. In fact, more often than not, positivism seemed to prove that such a foundation does not exist. A. Westermarck, for example, endeavored to use genetic theory and methodology to articulate a scientific basis for morality, and after several years of research produced three fat volumes that showed that there is, in fact, no such thing as morality. When values were uncovered, comparative analysis of various world cultures suggested (as Giambattista Vico had argued back in the early eighteenth century) that they are culturally based, that humans create their values, and there is nothing either eternal or natural at their core.

The increasing unconditional trust in science as an approach, coupled with its erosion of traditional values on the one hand and its inability to discover new ones on the other, created a vacuum of truth and meaning that threatened in the last quarter of the nineteenth century to shake popular confidence. However, the enthusiasm for science had a momentum, and it was only in certain intellectual pockets that anyone was really worried. But their worries intensified when some positivists argued that they had indeed discovered, through science, the actual foundations of human meaning, and then went on to claim that only the "survival of the fittest" directs our destiny. Social Darwinism became positivism's last chance for certainty but offered no law beyond the "law of the jungle."

BY THE TIME ALDOUS HUXLEY was attending the Garsington salon, the misapplication of evolutionary theory was having terrifying consequences, which galvanized Huxley's worries about the war and about science's ability to provide values.

Social Darwinists sought to apply the theory of the evolution of species to the circumstances of human cultures, i.e., politics, religion, economics, and social systems. The foundation of all their arguments was that since culture is a human product, different levels of human biological development produce different, but corresponding, cultural structures. So, for instance, cavemen had social structures and religions, but theirs were less "evolved" than ours because cavemen were less evolved biologically.

This idea was coupled with another idea: that there exists on the earth, at any given time, a range of different stages of human development. Some cultures are closer to those of the caveman and some are more progressive. Since Social Darwinists believed European cultures to be the most civilized, they believed them also to be the most evolved. The West therefore became the standard by which other civilizations could be measured. Herbert Spencer (1820-1903), Edward Burnett Tylor (1832-1917), and others argued that Native American, Native Australian, and Native African cultures were really living Europe's past. Eventually, these people would evolve further and then express that biological growth by recreating European culture, including its recent developments of capitalism and industrialization.

There are, of course, many flaws in their thesis. Darwin had simply argued that species that adapt to climatic change have a better chance of survival. He wasn't arguing that as they change they "improve" or progress in any specific direction or toward some platonic ideal of perfection. The direction of evolution is value free: the dinosaurs who survived the longest were not the moral and spiritual superiors of those who first became extinct.

Thomas Huxley had hoped the human race could use science to free itself of delusion—but the Social Darwinists used science, including some of Huxley's own thoughts, to justify a new delusion.

They insisted that the current European social, economic, and political structures were superior because, in the "struggle for existence," they were the ones that had survived. Conquerors, and entrepreneurs who "won" in the marketplace, had succeeded because their actions accorded best with nature's law; they were simply the most fit for survival. And those who lost out, the poor and "uncivilized," simply demonstrated by losing their lack of evolutionary fitness. Members of other races and cultures, not to mention the lower classes, were characterized as unfit for survival. In this way, Social Darwinism became not only a justification for class hierarchy, imperialism, racism, slavery, and patriarchy but also for the First World War. In the decade prior to the First World War, advocates of nationalism all over Europe borrowed ideas from Social Darwinism to glorify conflict and justify the subjugation of other people. "War," exclaimed the Prussian General von Bernhardi in 1911 in *Germany and the Next War*, "is a biological necessity of the first importance." The result of this new delusion was the most horrifying, barbaric, indecisive, and bloody war in human history.

SOCIAL DARWINISM'S EFFECT on many intellectuals, including Aldous Huxley, was an aggravated pessimism and a loss of confidence in the direction of society. Many saw European civilization as dying and beyond redemption. Aldous wrote in 1916, in his first book of poetry, "The West has plucked its flowers and has thrown them fading on the night," and TS. Eliot wrote in *The Wasteland:*

> What are the roots that clutch, what branches grow
> Out of this stony rubbish? Son of man,
> You cannot say, or guess, for you know only
> A heap of broken images.

There was pessimism at Garsington, and a loss of hope, but there were other things also, and some of them positive. There was a sober recognition of the moral and ideological bankruptcy of traditional values. This produced a sense of existential meaninglessness but it also produced freedom, for if traditional perspectives no longer held water then there was no need to follow them. As Huxley explained later: "For myself, as, no doubt, for many of my contemporaries, the philosophy of meaninglessness was essentially an instrument of liberation."

Garsington was therefore a place where freedom of thought and freedom of speech were not only encouraged but were demanded. New ideas and new modes of behavior, including sexual liberality, were the standards. This precipitated several love affairs—including one between Lady Ottoline and Bertrand Russell—and it was at Garsington that Aldous met his first wife, Maria. But beyond sexual license, the erosion of traditional values also opened up the possibility of a new artistic vision, and Lady Ottoline's salon was one of the cradles of the new trend in literature, with Huxley deeply involved in it.

Just after the middle of the nineteenth century, the dominant literary genre had been realism, a movement, in many ways, in opposition to the romantics' veneration of the inner life. Realists, perceiving romanticism to be too sentimental, and romantics to be too self-involved, sought to describe the outer life, the truth of the world around them, and modeled their approach on the scientific method. Poetry had been the primary literary form of the romantics but the novel better suited the purposes of realism. With an observant and clinical eye for detail, Turgenev described rural life in Russia, Harriet Beecher Stowe described the circumstances of racism and slavery in America, and Dickens described the consequences of capitalism and industrialism on English life. But at Garsington, and elsewhere, a new aesthetic was growing as a consequence of the loss of the traditional matrix of values and beliefs. These modernists argued that without this matrix there was nothing but habit and cultural momentum to unite artists and their public in a common sense of significance and value. Without an absolute truth or a shared absolute morality, many artists and writers came to believe that the only truths we can know for certain are those truths we experience in personal consciousness.

The modernists explored their interior lives and presented the interior lives of their characters and the pathology of their private worlds. As they threw off what they now perceived as the arbitrary boundaries of traditional values and morality (e.g., Victorian prudishness, blind praise of science, social structure for its own sake, and middle-class tastes), so they also wished to dispense with the conventional literary forms which conveyed them. In England, Arnold Bennett and H.G. Wells were the most successful novelists at the beginning of the twentieth century, but Virginia Woolf recoiled from the "materialism" of their attention to the exterior world. In the works of Joyce, Lawrence, Kafka, Woolf, Proust, and Huxley we find new structures based on how best to present the interior world. The stream of consciousness technique is the most famous, but Huxley, as we will see, developed his own approach.

IN 1916 HUXLEY GRADUATED from Oxford—one of only two receiving first honors in English that year—and was eager to get on with things, though it was not clear yet what those "things" would be. Writing wasn't paying the rent yet and he was exploring the possibility of a career in teaching. Directly after graduation he took a teaching post at Repton, in Derby, and the next winter he accepted a post at his old school, Eton. But Huxley missed his literary friends and found teaching boring. "It has its pleasant side, to be sure," he wrote Lewis Gielgud, "but also its tediousness." During his many visits to Garsington Huxley had found a more liberated side of himself, a personality free of the many constraints of class and family. He was tired of having to act the part of a Huxley and a British gentleman. He wrote from Eton to a friend: "I am always afraid of being made old by the continual assumption of superiority, the unceasing pretence of knowing better, of being respectable and a good example, which has to be kept up. I do my best to make my boys have no respect for me whatever."[5]

Eliot was then working for a literary journal, *The Egoist*, and Aldous hoped to find similar work. He was constantly worried about money during this period as he was hoping to marry Maria Nys, the daughter of a prosperous Belgian family who had to flee their homeland when the Germans invaded. Nys had arrived in England with her mother and two sisters, with only enough money to last them for two months. Many British families were taking in refugees and Lady Ottoline, through friends, offered Maria's mother hospitality for as long as she needed it. Mrs. Nys decided to send Maria, only sixteen at the time, but the oldest daughter, to Garsington. Aldous quickly took a liking to Nys and is said to have moped around terribly when she later left for Italy to join her family near Florence.

In January of 1919 he finally got the job that would make marriage possible. John Middleton Murry, another friend from Garsington, had taken over the editorship of the *Athenaeum* and offered Huxley a job. Aldous quickly accepted. The couple had been separated for more than two years, and now that the Germans had surrendered the previous November, Maria had returned to Belgium. Huxley would go there at Easter and ask for her hand in marriage.

Soon the couple was settled in London with Aldous slaving away at the *Athenaeum* (which he nonetheless enjoyed). He goes so far as to say in one letter that "it is in a way restful work," but this is difficult to imagine as he was running constantly to keep up with his responsibilities to job and family. In fact, during one eight month stretch in 1919, he wrote twenty-nine signed articles and one hundred and seventy-one notices and reviews for the *Athenaeum*, not to mention eight more articles for the *London Mercury*, and some reviews for the *Statesman*.

His new book of poetry, including the very long title poem, *Leda*, received favorable reviews but Huxley still had to do other work to survive. He and Maria had had a son that April—named Matthew after his great uncle, Matthew Arnold—and, with the added responsibility, Huxley took on another job as the drama critic for the *Westminster Gazette*. He wrote to Julian at the end of December: "Christmas for me is the blackest and bloodiest of seasons, as it means that I have to go to at least two and sometimes three theatres per diem and write about them afterwards. I am a total wreck in consequence." Huxley got a lot of material for his novels from these experiences as a journalist in London, but he also got sick and by late winter he was forced to take a work leave to restore his health.

He took off to Italy, first staying near Florence with friends (a family who had hosted Maria's family during the war), and then, as the weather warmed up, at the seaside at Forte de Marmi. Huxley loved the beach and thrived in the sunlight and heat, a pleasure he would also later enjoy in California. The product of this period of rejuvenation, besides his convalescence, was his first novel, *Crome Yellow*, written mostly in two months. It was set at a house party at a country estate named Crome Yellow, and was based on his experiences at Garsington. The novel was not a blockbuster but it sold quite well and certainly caught the attention of the intellectual community. Sybille Bedford, a friend of Huxley and his first biographer, remembers: "People were dazzled; he had made a name."[6]

*Crome Yellow* taught Huxley how productive he could be if he only had time to write, and so he applied himself to creating that time. Two years later, in 1923, based on his sales in prose (both from *Crome Yellow* and his second book of short stories, *Mortal Coils*), his publishers offered Huxley a continuing agreement. The contract demanded that Huxley give them two manuscripts per year, one of them a novel, for the next three years in exchange for a modest annual income. Huxley accepted, and the next fall saw the publication of one of his most important novels, *Antic Hay*.

In his early fiction Huxley often reflected on the time he had spent at the Garsington salon and in London just after the war. The second novel, *Antic Hay*, takes its name from a verse of playwright and poet. Christopher Marlowe: "My men like satyrs grazing on the lawns, Shall with their goat feet dance the antic hay." In *Antic Hay* Huxley describes the aimless lives of several intellectuals and artists after the war, ghosts who move through a moral vacuum. It is a dark book, ostensibly, and readers only familiar with the later, more mystical and optimistic Huxley, are usually surprised by its profound cynicism.

Huxley, true to the modernist perspective, believed that all individual human minds are subjective and therefore unique, mostly aware only of themselves. He believed their uniqueness has a tendency to make them isolated—which, in turn, makes love or intimate communication between individuals both difficult and unlikely. True to this perspective, in Huxley's early novels human relationships are

more commonly based on personal gain, hypocrisy, insecurity, mis-
understanding, or delusion than they are upon love. And even when
the characters think they understand each other, the reader is usually
subjected to the bitter irony of knowing better. For instance, in a rep-
resentative scene in *Antic Hay*, Lypiatt, a painter whose paintings no
one really likes, is talking with Myra Vivesh, once his lover but who
now can't believe she ever gave in to the dunce. She is humoring him
by letting him paint her portrait, during which time Lypiatt has a
moment of doubt about his work.

> He put down his palette, he stepped on to the dais,
> he came and knelt at Mrs. Vivesh's feet. He took
> one of her hands between his own and he bent over
> it, pressing it to his forehead, as though it were a
> charm against unhappy thoughts, sometimes kissing
> it; soon it was wet with tears. He wept almost in si-
> lence.
>
> "It's all right," Mrs. Vivesh kept repeating, "it's
> all right," and she laid her free hand on his bowed
> head, she patted it comfortingly as one might pat the
> head of a large dog that comes and thrusts its muz-
> zle between one's knees. She felt, even as she made
> it, how meaningless and unintimate the gesture was.
> If she had liked him, she would have run her fingers
> through his hair; but somehow his hair rather dis-
> gusted her. "It's all right, all right." But of course it
> wasn't all right; and she was comforting him under
> false pretenses and he was kneeling at the feet of
> somebody who simply wasn't there—so utterly de-
> tached, so far away she was from all this scene and
> all his misery.
>
> "You're the only person," he said at last, "who
> cares or under-stands."

If the circumstances weren't so sad and pathetic, Mrs. Vivesh
could almost have laughed. But ultimately it isn't funny, and this is

the bottom line on humor in Huxley's novels. His characters are often amusing but only sardonically so, and the joke, ultimately, is on us, the readers, for we are likewise trapped in a moral vacuum. At the end of the novel, Gumbril, the main character, whose affections for Mrs. Vivesh go unrequited, is seated beside her.

> "Tomorrow," said Gumbril at last, meditatively.
> "Tomorrow," Mrs. Vivesh interrupted him, "will be as awful as to-day."

Many readers, including his father, disliked Huxley's cynicism—but it became a source of confirmation and liberation to many in his generation. In Huxley they found a prophet, an "intellectual emancipator," who challenged traditional values and pointed up their dissatisfaction with hollow posturing and moral hypocrisy. He became a hero, an articulate voice for what Gertrude Stein called the "lost generation." Jocelyn Brooke, a critic writing about Huxley in 1954, explained, "For those who, like the writer of the present essay, were growing up during the nineteen twenties, Aldous Huxley seemed unquestionably the most stimulating and exciting writer of the day. By comparison, most other contemporary writers seemed stuffy, unenlightened and old fashioned."[7]

HUXLEY BOTH EXPRESSED AND crystallized the thinking of young intellectuals in his generation. He broke the silence—and he broke the mold. He wrote in the highest and most articulate prose but he expressed ideas and made statements that were, for his times, often unorthodox and politically incorrect. This only increased his popularity with his contemporaries. "When one was young," explained Kenneth Clark forty years later, "one read his books for their bright conversations, in which people said things that would have shocked one's schoolmasters."[8]

By today's standards many of the things Huxley was saying now seem tame, but it must be remembered that Huxley helped set today's standards. And there are still surprising allusions and comments for the modern reader—as when a character in *Antic Hay* tells his friends: "I remember, when I used to hang about the biological laboratories at school, eviscerating frogs—crucified with pins, they were, belly upward, like little green Christs."

Some critics dismissed him out of hand as merely a pessimist with a grudge against life. "Huxley's findings are always the same," wrote one. "Go where you will, do what you will, you will never escape from the smell of ordure and decay."[9] But Huxley was only describing what he saw; he wasn't endorsing it. He had felt tremendous loss in his personal life and, as an intellectual living after the war, could not help but feel, like the main character in Hermann Broch's *The Sleep Walkers,* "the icy breath sweeping over the world, freezing it to rigidity and withering all meaning out of things." But this does not mean Huxley was against all truths and all moral standards.

It is correct that his works contain a critical and sardonic view. It is also true that he was a cynic and an iconoclast. It is not true, however, that he proposed pessimism as life's answer and alternative. In fact, Huxley was disappointed with those who tried to use him to buttress this opinion. He wished they would see that his aim in criticizing the status quo was to suggest we try for something else. In *Those Barren Leaves*, Huxley's third novel, Mrs. Thriplow, a character who is also a writer, complains to a friend: "They like my books because they're smart and unexpected and rather paradoxical and cynical and elegantly brutal. They don't see how serious it all is. They don't see the tragedy and the tenderness underneath. . . . People seem to find it merely amusing, that's all."

Huxley was tearing things down—but he was tearing them down to build them up again. As the critic David Bowering has explained, in Huxley's novels, "the rejection of the corrupt society was always the first step to personal regeneration."[10]

Huxley never really let go of the Victorian view of social obligation. Like Arnold, he criticized the "Philistines," but also like Arnold, he wished to transcend criticizing and do something more. Much earlier, in 1915, in a letter to a friend, Aldous had explained that his mother, in her last letter, told him to be careful of being too critical of others ("a rather conceited and selfish fault of my own") and to "love much." He adds, "and I have come to see more and more how wise that advice was." Huxley hadn't abandoned his mother's advice or become irresponsible to it (nor would he ever be). One couldn't simply criticize. With the old values overturned, one had to find new ones and then lead the public to them. In *Jesting Pilate*, published in 1926, he explains, again in agreement with Arnold, that the artist, in this case, the writer, is important to "fill the vacuum created in the popular mind by the decay of established religion."

But one can't lead if one does not know the way, and Huxley, in the mid-twenties, was much more certain about what he didn't like, either for himself or his culture, than he was about what he did like. He understood the illness better than he understood the cure. That was the challenge—even with his own cynicism—and Huxley accepted it. As Clark later explained the development of Huxley's thought in his entry for *Aldous Huxley, A Memorial Volume,* edited by Julian: "Aldous might, as he did for some while, take it for granted that there was no meaning in the universe; yet once one had taken this for granted, it became more than an intellectual exercise of great fascination to construct a compass for the human voyage . . . to survive the voyage with mind intact."[11]

But what was the compass? Huxley would soon find his first real attempt at a direction in a close friendship with D. H. Lawrence. But for now his position was summed up in his disillusionment with science, in his belief that it could not provide meaning:

> The people of the West no longer share a literature and a system of ancient wisdom. All that they now have in common is science and information. Now, science is knowledge, not wisdom; deals with quantities, not with the qualities of which we are immediately aware. In as far as we are enjoying and suffering beings, its words seem to be mostly irrelevant and beside the point."[12]

Science's shortcomings, however, do not suggest to Huxley that meaning should therefore be abandoned. If science can't provide them we must simply find them elsewhere: "Our sense of values is intuitive. There is no proving the real existence of values in any way that will satisfy the logical intellect. Our standards can be demolished by argumentation; but we are none the less right to cling to them."[13]

# - 4 -

# D.H. LAWRENCE

*I have been defeated and dragged down by pain and worsted by
the evil world-soul of to-day. But still I know that life is for delight.*

— D.H. Lawrence

IN THE SPRING OF 1923 Aldous and Maria made a sudden departure for Italy, where they would live, primarily, for the next four
years. Aldous had enjoyed Italy the two previous summers, and especially the seacoast at Forte dei Marmi, and knew that with enough
freedom to write he could be very productive. However, he was hurried into his decision to move by the circumstances of a recent love
affair with Nancy Cunard, a poet and an heiress to the famous steamship line. Huxley had known Cunard for several years but in the fall
of 1922 he had somehow become overly infatuated with her. She was
flamboyant, wild, and in most other respects his opposite, which
perhaps attracted him. She was also deeply critical of "bourgeois hypocrisy," according to Allanah Harper, her biographer, and this was
certainly one of Aldous's favorite axes to grind. Whatever the basis of
the attraction, and most likely it was a mix of things, by winter Aldous was spending his evenings with Cunard and her entourage of
admirers and conspirators. In fact, Huxley himself became the prototype for several of his later characters, including Walter Bidlake from
*Point Counter Point*, modeled on his own pathetic behavior at the time.
"That poor, silly little Bidlake boy," observes another character. "Like
a rabbit in front of a weasel."

Aldous knew himself not to really be in love with Cunard, but he
had become obsessed with her sexual presence and her force-of-

nature personality. But the late nights took their toll on his often-frail constitution and, according to the account that Maria, his wife, later gave, one night she had simply had enough. When Aldous trudged in late one night, physically and emotionally wrecked, she told him she was resolved to go to Italy—right then—with or without him. She packed all night, with Aldous sitting glumly to the side watching. When morning came, Maria left. Aldous got up and dumbly followed. They headed directly to the train station and that was the end of London for a time—and the end of Cunard for good.

Huxley's affair had become intolerable to Maria not because of his sexual infidelity. After all, this was Fitzgerald's freewheeling "Jazz Age," the time of the flapper, and the Huxleys' own experiences at Garsington had convinced them that sexual openness was part of civilized behavior. Freud had argued compellingly that moral prohibitions do not negate our "evil" impulses but only repress them, driving them deeper into the psyche to fester into neurosis and illness, and it was part of Huxley's scientific rationalism at the time to believe him. The affair with Cunard became unbearable to Maria because it had consumed Aldous—he had a book due but he couldn't write—and this squandering of his talent, energy, and growth was what most infuriated her.

By the time they left for Italy Huxley had published, in addition to his fiction, a collection of essays and articles from his time as a journalist with the *Athenaeum* entitled *On the Margin*. Writing essays came naturally to Aldous, and soon after his return to Italy he became interested in writing travel essays. Consequently, in 1924, the Huxleys bought a car and began a series of road trips throughout Europe. The first trip was mainly in Italy and resulted in his book *Along the Road*, published a year later.

Aldous liked cars, first buying a Citroen and later, when he could afford it, a custom-built Bugatti. He, of course, couldn't drive though. Maria, though small and slight, did all the driving—and had a reputation for being good at it. But Huxley liked to travel, and not just because he became enamored of whizzing around in cars (which he did), but also because it gave him a congenial means of fulfilling his demanding book contracts; he could do "research" for them while going off on long holidays. Huxley wasn't shirking his duty as a writer though. After he caught the travel bug he simply applied it to his intrinsic curiosity of the world and everything in it, using the "bug" to produce some engrossing essays, not only on travel but also on the art, the architecture, and the history he whizzed by along the way.

In 1925, just after the publication of *Along the Road,* Aldous and Maria took a much longer and more complex journey—sailing from Genoa around the world. They made many points of call including, eventually, the United States, but their travel plans focused on India and the Far East. This trip, lasting nine months, would result in the 1926 publication of his second travel book, *Jesting Pilate,* and would confirm him as a voyager for the rest of his life. Virginia Woolf once spoke in a letter about his penchant for getting around, lightly speculating that his near blindness might be the cause: "Aldous astounds me—his energy, his modernity. Is it that he can't see anything that he has to see so much?"[1]

Travel writing also gave Aldous a respite from writing fiction. It wasn't that Huxley had come to dislike fiction; he had merely come to dislike his fiction. He wished to write a novel that would truly matter artistically, which for Huxley meant pointing in a moral direction, but he was having trouble doing so. In a letter to his father, in April 1924, he explained that he had just finished his third book of short stories but that the "mere business of telling a story interests me less and less." He went on to add that he had begun a novel he hoped would do more. But the novel, *Those Barren Leaves,* didn't do more, at least not in Huxley's own eyes. He wrote to a friend in 1925 that the book was "all right, certainly; tremendously accomplished, but in a queer way, I now feel, jejune and shallow and off the point. All I've written so far has been off the point. And I've taken such enormous pains to get off it; that's the stupidity. All this fuss in the intellectual void . ."[2]

HUXLEY DOUBTED HIMSELF as an artist. Of course, he hadn't really wanted to be an artist in the first place, and sometimes he grumbled at being forced off the track of his earlier interests. In *Along the Road* he says that if he could choose his next existence he'd become what he'd hoped to be as a boy, a scientist. "The only thing that might make me hesitate would be an offer by fate of artistic genius. But even if I could be Shakespeare, I think I should still choose to be Faraday."

Huxley recognized that his particular strength lay in the rational function of his mind. In many ways he had the proclivities and demeanor of a college professor or a philosopher. In fact, as early as 1918 in *The Defeat of Youth*, in his poem "The Life Theoretic," he had observed:

> But I who think about books and such—
> I crumble to impotent dust before the struggling,
> And the women palsy me with fear.
> But when it comes to fumbling over books and thinking about
>      God and the Devil and all,
> Why, there I am.

But his intellectual strength was also, in his eyes, a weakness holding him back from the world around him, and keeping him distracted in his own musings. From very early on he perceived this as a personal shortcoming that he wished to transcend, and in *The Defeat of Youth* he also writes:

> I scorned all fire that outward of the eyes
> Could kindle passion; scorned, yet was afraid;
> Feared, and yet envied those more deeply wise
> Who saw the bright earth beckon and obeyed.

True to his Arnold side, Aldous believed that the artist more than the philosopher or scientist could lead civilization forward. Artists transcend the mono-dimensionality of the strictly logical or intellectual. They have the potential to get beyond the abstractions implicit to philosophy. And because they experience more widely they can also present more deeply to an audience. Reason had led Huxley to this conclusion but now he wished to leave reason behind, to embrace what was beyond reason and from that experience to create a deeper art.

Up to this time, ironically and, for Huxley, frustratingly, his art was composed to a significant extent by rational devices constructed to deliver an aesthetic effect. His novels dripped with irony, but the tool for creating it was mechanical in nature. What Huxley was doing was sharply contrasting two viewpoints of the same circumstances. David Bowering has called these Huxley's "linked incompatibles," and another critic, Milton Birnbaum, has observed that they create irony because they "present life as a mix of mutually contradictory states."[3] In his 1931 essay "Wanton Optics," from *Music at Night*, Huxley himself explained the method: "Juxtapose two accounts of the same human event, one in terms of pure science, the other in terms of religion, aesthetics, passion, even common sense; their discord will set up the most disquieting reverberations in the mind."

A good example of this device that predates his explanation of it is in his most famous short story, "The Gioconda Smile," from *Mortal Coils,* published in 1922. True to the modernist spirit, Huxley presents a lack of communication between two of his characters; specifically, Mr. Hutton is making love absentmindedly to the mistress with whom he's become bored:

> He kissed her again, whispering her name several times: Doris, Doris, Doris. The scientific appellation of the sea-mouse, he was thinking as he kissed the throat she offered him, white and extended like the throat of a victim awaiting the sacrificial knife. The sea-mouse was a sausage with iridescent fur: very peculiar. Or was Doris the sea-cucumber, which turns itself inside out in moments of alarm? He would really have to go to Naples again, just to see the aquarium. These sea creatures were fabulous, unbelievably fantastic.
>
> "Oh, Teddy Bear!" (More zoology; but he was only a land animal. His poor little jokes!) "Teddy Bear, I'm so happy."
>
> "So am I," said Mr. Hutton.

Huxley's fans thrilled over his techniques and his wicked ironies but Aldous felt confined by his approach. Much later, in 1945, Huxley explained in a letter that he was "not congenitally a novelist" and was therefore "compelled to resort to devices which the born novelist would never think of using." In *Point Counter Point,* published in 1928, Huxley exhibited his frustration over this in a memory that his character Philip Quarles, an overly intellectual novelist based on Huxley himself, has about one of his wife's comments: "'Ah, if you were a little less of an overman, Phil,' she used to say, 'what good novels you'd write!' Rather ruefully he agreed with her. He was intelligent enough to know his own defects."

HUXLEY WAS LOOKING to break out, both as a person and as an artist, and he was exploring various ways to do so. This became an ongoing project in his life, but in the mid-1920s he found his first "way" through a friendship with D.H. Lawrence.

David Herbert Lawrence was born on September 11, 1885, in a mining village in Nottinghamshire. His father was a miner and an alcoholic; his mother was intelligent and encouraged his education. Lawrence eventually won several scholarships and, like Huxley, worked for a time as a schoolteacher—but unlike Huxley, he had formally trained for the job. However, Lawrence's interests in writing—along with a period of significant illness—carried him away from teaching, and in 1910 he published his first novel, *The White Peacock,* at the age of twenty-five. It was *The Rainbow,* however, published five years later that established his reputation as a libertine, an iconoclast, and a sensualist. *The Rainbow* was considered so blatantly sexual that it was banned in England for many years. Lawrence, of course, was not dissuaded. In fact, the censors convinced him he was onto something important and so he continued to write in the same vein.

Lawrence enjoyed traveling and was always on the lookout for a place to establish "Rananim," his name for a proposed small colony of liberal and like-minded people—what Huxley later called his "colony of escape." His companion on these travels was Frieda, a German whom he had met in Nottingham while she was still the wife of a professor there. Frieda left her husband and her two children to be with Lawrence and, after she had secured a divorce, they were married in 1914. Frieda is infamous in Lawrence's biographies for being both his inspiration and, at least partially, his ruin. Most sources characterize her as devoted to Lawrence but also overly flighty and impractical. Even Maria, who had a reputation for being generous, once observed in frustration: "Frieda is silly. She is like a child, but Lawrence likes her because she is a child."

Huxley had first met Lawrence in 1915, in London. Lawrence had invited Aldous to tea on the recommendation of Lady Ottoline Morrell, a patron of Lawrence's to whom he dedicated *Amores*, a book of poems. Although Huxley and Lawrence never met at Garsington, they still met because of it. Lawrence's own visits to Garsington eventually became the substance of *Women in Love*, and the presence of Frieda at Garsington was partially what gave it the reputation of being a haven for German spies.

After Huxley and Lawrence's first meeting they lost contact for a time, but in 1926, while Aldous was still in India, he received a letter from Lawrence praising his travel essays of Italy and suggesting a meeting between them when Huxley returned. Aldous was well aware of Lawrence's work and reputation. Intrigued, he dropped in on Lawrence that October while in Florence to see his dentist. The two men quickly became close and remained so until Lawrence's death in 1930.

Positivists were still holding out for the day when science and reason would uncover the foundations of absolute truth and meaning; other rationalists held on to the view that science suggests there are no roots to truth and meaning. However, a third choice, growing in the late nineteenth and early twentieth centuries—a trend often referred to as irrationalism—disagreed with both perspectives. Friedrich Nietzsche, Henri Bergson, and Georges Sorel, two generations before Huxley, had argued that reason is not the primary function of the human mind and that science is not capable of judging whether life has meaning or not. In common, they argued that human behavior is more often directed by such nonrational forces as instincts, inspirations, drives, emotions, impulses and desires. These natural forces, which are as much a part of us as the intellect, lead us to a deeper truth than science. Consequently, Nietzsche argued that we should stop drowning and encumbering the other dimensions of ourselves in order to live a more authentic existence. Once in touch with the dark, mysterious levels within us we will know better who we are and what life is. Freud disagreed with Nietzsche with respect to the supremacy of the nonrational functions—and, in fact, hoped to use reason to better control them—hut his studies lent credibility to the idea that these irrational forces exist and strongly influence our behavior.

Nietzsche inspired Lawrence, as John Worthen has described in his biography of Lawrence's early years, and so did irrationalism in general. In *Psychoanalysis and the Unconscious*, published in 1921, and *Fantasia of the Unconscious*, published a year later, Lawrence articulated what can loosely be called his philosophy, though for obvious reasons he didn't care exactly how much logical sense it made. Lawrence warns in both books that he'll stay more true to his solar plexus than to the constraints of logic, a position he had held for several years. "My great religion," he wrote to a friend in 1912, "is a belief in the blood, the flesh, as being wiser than the intellect. We can go wrong in our minds. But what our blood feels and believes and says, is always true. The intellect is only a bit and bridle. What do I care about knowledge? All I want is to answer to my blood, direct, without fribbling intervention of mind, or moral, or whatever."[4]

Lawrence advocated a transcendence of Apollonian order and an embrace of Dionysus, Pan, and the other gods of instinct. He didn't believe in God per se, that is, in God as an exterior phenomenon, but he admired in the early Greek religion its broad pantheon, which, as he saw it, represented the full range of human emotions and psychological states. In addition to gods of intellect, there were also gods of desire, anger, and envy. Dark gods as well as light gods. Lawrence wore a satyr's beard and tutored that we must strike a balance between our dark and light sides, the "animal" and the "human" sides, to reconcile the body with the mind. Only then can we live fully and authentically. As Huxley later explained Lawrence's view in his important 1936 essay on Lawrence in *The Olive Tree:* "Man is an animal that thinks. To be a first rate human being, a man must be both a first-rate animal and a first-rate thinker (and, incidentally, he cannot be a first-rate thinker, at any rate about human affairs, unless he is also a first-rate animal)."

From the positivist perspective, Lawrence's view was in many ways indistinguishable from that of the existentialists. Both seemed to believe that life was meaningless. But for Lawrence there was an important difference: though he was saying that life has no absolute intellectual meaning, and that life is ultimately pointless, he claimed that life still had meaning and value if lived fully, in all its dimensions. "There is no point. Life and love are life and love, a bunch of wild violets is a bunch of wild violets, and to drag in the idea of a point is to ruin everything. Live and let live, love and let love, flower and fade, and follow the natural curve, which flows on, pointless."[5]

Lawrrence's viewpoint, "life-worshipping," as he called it, was compelling to Aldous, not only because it described a truth beyond science and the intellect but because it also opened up a door for the artist. Nietzsche had written in *Thus Spake Zarathustra*: "There is more rationality in thy body than in thy best wisdom. . . Of all that is written, I love only what a person hath written with his blood. Write with blood, and thou wilt find that blood is spirit." Huxley found himself believing this was so and Lawrence seemed to he proving it in his vivid novels.

Lawrence's views also appealed to the moralist in Huxley—perhaps intensified after his aimless affair with Nancy Cunard. Lawrence convinced Aldous that nihilism and hedonism, two malaises of their generation, were curable and were only the direct by-product of people's culturally programmed imbalance of body and mind. Since people had been taught that only the intellect could know truth, they had settled, thanks to science, into meaninglessness. And since they were cut off from their other dimensions of self, those aspects had deteriorated and reverted to primitiveness. This is what had caused their sexual promiscuity and general lasciviousness. In *Point Counter Point* Huxley puts Lawrence's ideas into the mouth of one of his outspoken characters, Rampion, who explains, ". . . it's the oppressed

D.H. Lawrence

(Corbis Collection)

body and instincts against the intellect. The intellect's been exalted as the spiritual upper classes; the spiritual lower classes rebel." So, if people would get in touch with their animal sides and balance them with their intellects, they would become cured. They would live a new life, a natural life, which has an implicit morality.

HUXLEY WAS ENTHUSIASTIC about Lawrence's perspective and helped to promote it. Literary critics commonly point out that it is in *Point Counter Point*, with the character Mark Rampion, that Huxley presented his first "good man," a character preaching a truth worth listening to and who is not presented satirically. Huxley also argued for Lawrence's viewpoint cogently in his next two books of essays, *Proper Studies*, published in 1927, and *Do What You Will*, published two years later.

Lawrence and Huxley became very close friends—in fact, Richard Aldington, a friend of Lawrence and his first biographer, explains that during the last five years of Lawrence's life, Huxley was his closest friend. This is true but it still surprises, simply because they were so very different. They came from different classes and family backgrounds. And their personalities differed broadly. Huxley was quiet and withdrawn; Lawrence was passionate and extroverted. Lawrence was nine years older and more confirmed in his irrationalism. Huxley was by nature doubting and cerebral, while Lawrence was prophetic—"in touch," as Huxley said later, "with unknown modes of being." However, they did have a great many views in common—and they also each had a passion for ranting in support of those views.

Both men had a tendency to engage in what Lawrence called "grizzling," that is, complaining about the current state of things. As a child Aldous had been fond of grumbling. So much so that his family once had given him a milk mug which read: "Oh, isn't the world extremely flat, With nothing whatever to grumble at." (He would eventually learn to heed the warning his mother had later given him to be careful of his tendency to criticize.) Lawrence also enjoyed a good rant, as his letters amply attest (he wrote to a friend in 1928: "How I hate the attitude of ordinary people to life. How I loathe ordinariness! How from my soul I abhor nice simple people, with their eternal price-list. It makes my blood boil."). One finds it easy—especially when reading *Do What You Will*, a book of essays, where Huxley sometimes gets up on his high horse (for example, in "Silence Is Golden," an essay about his disdain for talking films)—to believe that the two men sometimes found a common passion in "grizzling" about society and culture. They railed that Christianity had taught humans to abhor their bodies and to see the world as an inferior place, as a way station. They railed that philosophy had been created mainly from fear, from a need to know and control, and was chaining us to live in abstractions. And they railed that science had stolen imagination from the world and given it industrialization in its place. "It's Jesus' and Newton's and Henry Ford's disease," Rampion, the Lawrence figure, rants in *Point Counter Point.* "Between them, the three have pretty well killed us. Ripped the life out of our bodies and stuffed us with hatred."

Lawrence and Huxley agreed on all these points, but the difference between them, as Huxley often remarked, was that "his opinions are lived and mine, in the main, only thought." Huxley had reached his conclusions rationally, rather than by touching his inner animal. In fact, Huxley embraced Lawrence's viewpoint because it made sense to him—and this irony placed him, in his own mind, in an inferior position to Lawrence. In *Point Counter Point* Philip Quarles, the overly intellectual novelist, writes in his journal about Rampion, the Lawrence figure:

> Being with Rampion rather depresses me; for he makes me see what a great gulf separates the knowledge of the obvious from the actual living of it. And oh, the difficulties of crossing that gulf! I perceive now that the real charm of the intellectual life—the life devoted to erudition, to scientific research, to philosophy, to esthetics, to criticism—is its easiness. It's the substitution of simple intellectual schemata for the complexities of reality. . .

And he later adds to this, "If I could only capture something of his secret."

BY THE TIME HUXLEY had reaffirmed their friendship Lawrence had returned from recent travels in Ceylon, Australia, Mexico, and Taos, New Mexico, and was already seriously ill, sick with the disease that would kill him in just four years. Lawrence had grown up in a mining village, one legacy of which was a tendency toward respiratory infections. He had from birth been subject to coughs, colds, bouts of flu, and bronchitis, and then, in 1901, while working as a clerk in a factory, he had contracted pneumonia. Lawrence later remarked that he never really recovered from that illness. In 1911 he nearly died of lung infection. However, despite Lawrence's illness, he and Huxley spent much time together—usually in company with their wives— first at Florence but also at Forte dei Marmi, Bandol, Paris, Chexbres, and eventually at Vence where Lawrence died.

For both Huxley and Lawrence the most memorable time together was a winter spent at Diablerets, Switzerland, and the events of that trip are significant for what they reveal about their relationship and its influence on Aldous.

On Christmas day in 1927, Aldous and Maria drove to Scandicci, Italy, to pick up Lawrence and Frieda and take them on a long holiday. Lawrence had written to say that he wanted to "eat turkey and be silly." Huxley also needed a break. He was having trouble with his fourth novel and he needed a rest. He was looking forward to spending time with Lawrence and, moreover, with his brother, Julian, who would also be at Diablerets.

While in the mountains, the men wrote in the mornings and in the afternoons they relaxed or took excursions. Lawrence later reminisced how he had particularly enjoyed a sleigh ride to the top of a mountain pass for a picnic. It had been a cold but beautiful day. In the evenings they talked about ideas and discussed their work. Lawrence was finishing his manuscript for *Lady Chatterley's Lover* and he let Aldous be its first reader. Huxley was impressed with it and Maria typed up a copy for the publishers from Lawrence's handwritten text.

Later, when the book became banned, Huxley championed it; he also helped Lawrence fight the pirated editions that soon cropped up. During those weeks at Diablerets, Huxley himself was working on *Point Counter Point*, the novel that would cement his reputation as an important novelist.

The evenings were often congenial but sometimes the discussions became difficult. The Huxley brothers enjoyed long and complex talks on scientific issues, and these conversations drove Lawrence crazy. He favored instinct and intuition and railed against the overly analytic or scientific—particularly with regards to evolutionary theory (a favorite of the Huxleys for obvious reasons, and especially with Julian already working on the research that would lead in 1942, to his book *Evolution: The Modern Synthesis*, the first post-Mendelian analysis of evolution as a process), which Lawrence entirely disbelieved. "His anger was particularly directed against myself, as a professional scientist," Julian later wrote in his *Memories*. "I learnt to disregard his outbursts of fury, but we had many stormy passages."[6]

Julian had just published *Religion Without Revelation*, in which he took up Thomas Huxley's other task of convincing the public that morality and science are not incompatible. In the book Julian argued that "man is not under the control or guidance of any supernatural Being or beings, but has to rely on himself and his own powers." This, ostensibly, agreed perfectly with Lawrence's humanism, and yet Lawrence viewed it as largely a continuation of the cultural habit to "make sense" of things. Julian's "religion in the light of science" was still a religion that kept the intellect in charge, so even if there were points Lawrence could agree with, the project, in general, was irksome to him. Furthermore, it bothered him that Aldous subscribed to all this scientific claptrap. In *Point Counter Point* Huxley shows Rampion accusing Philip Quarles of "whoring after abstractions," and certainly this may have been a direct comment from Lawrence. He grew frustrated with Aldous's intellectualism. "You are not your grandfather's *Enkel* for nothing—that funny dry-mindedness," he once wrote in a letter after reading Aldous's *Proper Studies*, a book of essays published in 1927.

Huxley wondered if Lawrence himself didn't err toward imbalance. Yes, certainly, the instincts and impulses must be given their due, but did that mean reducing the intellect to nothing at all? Maybe Lawrence had swung the pendulum too far. Huxley later wrote, in *Beyond the Mexique Bay,* published in 1934, "Lawrence so much hated the misapplications of science, that he thought that science should be abolished." Huxley didn't see how this was possible. On the practical level, on the level of technology, Huxley held, as he argued in *Do What You Will* that despite the negative consequences of applied science, "the machines must stay." To do otherwise would be criminal:

> There are twice as many human beings today as there were a hundred years ago. The existence of this increased population is dependent on the existence of modern machinery. If we scrap the machinery, we kill at least half the population. . . . No, the slaughter of nine hundred million human beings is not a piece of practical politics.

But even if science's applications could somehow be scrapped, should its facts be abolished too? Huxley couldn't see how this was a balance between mind and body. In his essay on Lawrence in *The Olive Tree*, he later wrote:

> His dislike of science was passionate and expressed itself in the most fantastically unreasonable terms. "All scientists are liars," he would say, when I brought up some experimentally established fact, which he happened to dislike. "Liars, Liars!" It was a most convenient theory. I remember in particular one long and violent argument on evolution, in the reality of which Lawrence always passionately disbelieved. "But look at the evidence, Lawrence," I insisted, "look at the evidence." His answer was characteristic. "But I don't care about the evidence. Evidence doesn't mean anything to me. I don't feel it *here*." And he pressed his two hands on his solar

plexus. I abandoned the argument and thereafter never, if I could avoid it, mentioned the hated name of science in his presence.

This was sometimes difficult for Huxley, and especially with regard to the circumstances of Lawrence's own health. In the last years of his life Lawrence was subject to bronchial hemorrhages and pleurisy. Huxley had made a point of researching his condition and understood it well. He became convinced that it was curable and later wrote that he believed it was "unnecessary, the result simply of the man's strange obstinacy against professional medicine." Lawrence didn't want to see the "liars" or visit their hospitals, and his wife, the flamboyant and childlike Frieda, reinforced this obstinacy in him, and so, according to Huxley, he drifted from place to place hoping somehow to outrun his disease. Huxley once wrote to Julian expressing his frustration: "He rationalizes the fear in all kinds of ways which are, of course, quite irrelevant. And meantime he just wanders about, very tired and at bottom wretched, from one place to another, imagining that the next place will make him feel better."

And yet Huxley always found it within him to take Lawrence, whose art he deeply admired, as he was. "He might propose impractical schemes," he wrote in *The Olive Tree*, "he might say or write things that were demonstrably incorrect or even, on occasion (as when he talked about science) absurd. But to a very considerable extent it didn't matter. What mattered was always Lawrence himself, was the fire that burned within him, that glowed with so strange and marvelous a radiance in almost all he wrote."

In July of 1929 Aldous realized how ill Lawrence was becoming and wrote to Julian: "It's pathetic to see the way he just sits and does nothing. He hasn't written a line or painted a stroke for the last three months." But Lawrence still did not want the doctor. "We have given up trying to persuade him to be reasonable. He doesn't want to be and nobody can persuade him to be—except possibly Frieda. But Frieda is worse than he is. We've told her that she's a fool and a criminal; but it has no more effect than telling an elephant."[7]

For some time Lawrence kept going "like a flame burning on in miraculous disregard of the fact that there was no more fuel to justify its existence," wrote Aldous. But by winter "the miracle was at the end" and Lawrence was failing. He was living in Vence, in the south of France, and had become so sick that he had allowed himself to be taken to a rest home. He wrote to Maria on February 21, 1930, "This place no good," and the Huxleys, realizing the end might be near, packed at once, leaving Bandol where they were staying to travel to Vence, arriving on the twenty-fourth. They found Lawrence "terribly changed," and during the next week his condition deteriorated further. The Huxleys stood by the bed daily and Maria, who was very close to Lawrence, wept openly. Lawrence asked that Frieda's bed be placed next to his and Aldous rearranged the furniture.

Finally, on March 2, Lawrence ran out of strength. At nine in the evening Aldous ran for the doctor; Lawrence was in so much pain that he had asked for morphine. The drug was given and it relaxed him. Soon he fell asleep. Maria held him in her arms and Frieda held his feet. Aldous sat beside the bed. Shortly after ten, he died. ("He went so quietly at the last," Aldous wrote to Julian the next day.) Lawrence's body was kept in the room until the following day when it was taken out for the funeral. Robert Nichols, a friend of Huxley and Lawrence, later described in a letter the scene as Lawrence's coffin was removed: "Aldous was standing absolutely impassive . . . His face was beautiful—and there was so to speak a marvelous pianissimo in it. Maria seemed in a dream and the big tears rolled two at a time down towards her nostrils." Frieda wore a red dress that day as the company followed a horse-drawn hearse to the gravesite. No words were spoken at the grave and no service was given. Lawrence was free.


HUXLEY HELPED TIE UP some of Lawrence's affairs and later compiled and edited his letters for publication. There is no doubt that he loved Lawrence deeply, and that he respected his viewpoint. "He was really, I think," Huxley wrote to Eugene Saxton a month after the funeral, "the most extraordinary and impressive human being I have ever known."[8]

His time with Lawrence solidified Huxley's conviction that truth must be of this world and that spirituality must include the physical, and that a full and meaningful life cannot be lived in either the imagination or the abstractions of the intellect alone. This legacy remained with Aldous all his life. Aldous was, however, too much of a Huxley not to allow science its due. Facts were facts and must be acknowledged; one couldn't just make up one's own reality and go live in it. He had always been critical of the romantics for trying to do just that. Huxley understood, as he once admitted, why Keats had cursed Newton for explaining the mechanics of the rainbow and thereby diminishing our sense of wonder. He understood why Blake had prayed to be delivered from "single vision and Newton's sleep." But he also understood that not liking the facts does not invalidate them or make them go away. A meaningful truth must include the human instincts but that does not dictate that it should not also make sense. The ultimate balance that Huxley was looking for was more of the Arnold than of the Lawrence kind, with an acknowledgement of what science could do as well as of what it could not do. In July of 1961 John Chandos interviewed Aldous in London for the BBC. While speaking about D.H. Lawrence, Huxley speculated that he could have used more balance with reason and that he was, in a sense, guilty of the narrowness he accused science of:

> The point is that you must have both. The blood and the flesh are there—and in certain respects they are wiser than the intellect. I mean if we interfere with the blood and the flesh with our conscious minds we get psychosomatic trouble. But on the other hand, we have to do a lot of things with the conscious mind. I mean why can't we do both—we *have* to do both. This is the whole art of life: making the best of all worlds. Here again [in Lawrence] is one of those fatal examples of trying to make everything conform to the standard of only *one* world. Seeing that we are amphibians—it's no good.

Huxley wished to enliven all his dimensions, as he tutored his readers to do, but he was still having trouble getting beyond his intellect. Lawrence was able to live his philosophy but he wasn't able, at least for Aldous, to provide a program by which others could live it—a program for contacting the "dark blood." When Huxley listened to his inner voices he couldn't help but weigh them in the light of his intellect, the stronger voice, which always remained skeptical. Hence he writes on the first page of *Do What You Will* that he is "officially an agnostic," though he went on to argue the Lawrence perspective. He could believe in things but he could only do so provisionally. This was, as he saw it, both his strength and his weakness. Philip Quarles, the Huxley character in *Point Counter Point*, says of himself in his notebook:

> Against the pyrrhonian suspense of judgment and the stoical imperturbability he had often rebelled. But had the rebellion ever been really serious? . . . always, whatever he might do, he knew quite well in the secret depths of his being that he wasn't a Catholic, or a strenuous liver, or a mystic or a noble savage. And although he sometimes nostalgically wished he were one or other of these things, or all of them at once, he was always secretly glad to be none of them, and at liberty, even though his liberty was in a strange paradoxical way a handicap and a confinement to his spirit.[9]

What Aldous was saying was that his transcendence, if it came, would have to wait.

# - 5-

## BRAVE NEW WORLD

*If a nation expects to be ignorant and free,*
*it expects what never was and never will be.*
—Thomas Jefferson

IN APRIL OF 1930, THE MONTH AFTER Lawrence died, the Huxleys moved into a house they had bought in a fishing village on the French Riviera at Sanary. Speaking French was not a problem for either Aldous or Maria, who both spoke it fluently and, in fact, carried on their personal relationship in French. They had been living near Paris for most of the past two years to be closer to where their son, Matthew, was attending school, but they had missed the seashore and the quiet country environment. Aldous was doing better financially, and they purchased a modest whitewashed house with green shutters in a landscape of hills, farms, pastures, and olive trees.

When they arrived to move in, they found that a worker, hoping to please them, had painted "Villa Huley" on the gateposts in bright green letters. Aldous found the misspelling comical and kept the name as it was. Aldous had a studio built for himself and kept to his writing, but he also had taken up painting. Lawrence had been a writer who extolled the virtues of painting, and Huxley seems to have found it both enjoyable and therapeutic. Maria kept the house and, as always, watched over Aldous, protecting his time and his privacy. In her bedroom she kept a large painting that Lawrence had done.

*Point Counter Point* had been a great success and financed the new home. The novel sold twenty thousand copies in the first year, and the critical reviews for the book were excellent. Huxley was writing "novels of ideas," in which characters became spokesmen for certain views that were then juxtaposed to create irony and dramatic effect. *Crome Yellow* and *Those Barren Leaves* were consciously written after the style of Thomas Love Peacock, who set his novels in the rooms and gardens of country estates, and who also wrote, as did Huxley, primarily for and about intellectuals. Even in *Antic Hay* and the much longer novel *Point Counter Point* Huxley provides a minimum of plot and a minimum of character development. The characters are essentially notions and dispositions set up on legs. The critic, Harold H. Watt, once remarked that in *Crome Yellow* there was only enough happening "to keep the characters talking and no more." Plot was not the point and, of course, not everyone was used to that idea. In fact, once, in July of 1926, when Virginia Woolf went to meet Thomas Hardy, who was then eighty-six, Hardy mentioned that his wife was reading him a collection of Huxley's stories; when asked for comment he laughed and said, "We used to think there was a beginning and a middle and an end."[1]

But most critics did not find Huxley's approach defective. Anthony Burgess, best known today for his novel *A Clockwork Orange*, once said that Huxley had "equipped the novel with a brain."[2] However, there was a limitation in this approach and Huxley was keenly aware of it. "The chief defect of the novel of ideas," says Philip Quarles, the intellectual novelist in *Point Counter Point*, "is that you must write about people who have ideas to express—which excludes all but about .01 per cent of the human race."

However successful *Point Counter Point* was though (it has remained continuously in print), it fell short of Huxley's goal in at least one respect. It was still largely cynical in content and, despite the brief recommendations for a better life spouted by Mark Rampion (the mouthpiece for Lawrence's ideas), it continued Huxley's portrayal of a disillusioned generation.

Lawrence had applauded the novel and wrote to Huxley that he believed Aldous had given the best portrait of his generation, but the undercurrent of the letter seems to ask, "So what's next?"

The answer was that Aldous didn't know. He still hadn't found the deeper, experiential truth he was looking for, the truth beyond ideas from which he hoped to speak as a novelist. He was still most comfortable only in his intellectual skepticism. As Robert Baker, editor of Huxley's *Collected Essays* (2000), says, "By the end of the decade [the 1920s) he was fond of referring to himself as a Pyrronist, that is, a thinker who mistrusts all philosophical systems founded on notions of essential truth." Pyrrho, the Greek philosopher, had advocated a suspension of judgment on all matters involving an absolute truth claim. But to be a Pyrrhonist, an agnostic about all truths (not just the religious ones), did not exclude Huxley from exploring the possibilities. He still believed that Lawrence had made some important insights into meaning, and he still believed that the artist was needed to lead society to a higher set of values. In his own art he had gone about as far in *Point Counter Point* as his artistic vision could lead him—which was far enough for his readers but not far enough for Huxley.

While he was waiting to find a deeper inspiration, and resting from the effort of writing so complex a novel as *Point Counter Point,* Huxley would set his mind to another way to serve society. He would write essays of social and literary criticism. And here his career almost exactly replicated that of his granduncle Matthew Arnold. In the 1860s Arnold had begun writing social and literary criticism when he had become dissatisfied with what he could express in poetry. There also are strong similarities between the two authors with regard to their hope about the powers of art.

Arnold believed that art and culture represented society's most effective means of elevating itself out of meaninglessness and vulgarity. In the first chapter of *Culture and Anarchy* he explains that the civilized mind is characterized by its qualities of "sweetness and light." He arrives at this phrase by borrowing from Jonathan Swift's conclusions in *The Battle of the Books,* contrasting two insects, a bee and a spider. The spider represented for Arnold, as for Swift, the narrow-minded and uncultured perspective, which sits self-satisfied in the web of its own delusion. On the other hand, the bee represented the cultured mind, which roams free and collects the raw material that can then be made into honey and wax. Arnold liked Swift's conclusion, that since candles can be made from wax, the bee supplies humanity with "the two noblest of things, which are sweetness and light." Arnold took up the phrase, and the viewpoint, and went on to articulate, in many essays, how art and culture could cure the ills of a sick society.

In broad outline, Huxley's program, as he drew it in the five books of essays he wrote between 1929 and 1936 (a period in which he produced only one novel), differs very little from Arnold's. In *The Olive Tree* he sometimes almost perfectly echoes Arnold's general viewpoint. He tells us that great books "give form and direction to our experience. And at the same time they provide experience of a new kind, intense, pure, unalloyed with irrelevance." Great literature is a medicine. "The verbal universe is at once a mould for reality and a substitute for it, a superior reality. And what props the mind, what shores up its impending ruin, is contact with this superior reality of ordered beauty and significance."[3]

Huxley also advocated "sweetness and light" as a cure for social ills. And also like Arnold, he asserted that only because literature has a practical effect in its influence on society is it really worthwhile. Neither Arnold nor Huxley believed in the adage of "art for art's sake," made famous by Oscar Wilde. Art is a means not an end. Art, if it has no moral purpose, is empty and therefore vulgar for both men. Great books can "modify the character of those who read them," wrote Huxley, and that is their best purpose: to take advantage of what the French philosopher, Jules de Gaultier, has said is one of the essential faculties of the human being—"the power granted to man to conceive himself as other than he is."

The similarities between Arnold and Huxley's programs are not limited to their views of art as a path to morality and meaning; they are also similar when they describe the specific ills of society that art must cure. Both men believed that capitalism and industrialization were creating a culture of Philistines who threatened to overturn the apple-cart of civilization. Understanding these Philistines is important for understanding Huxley's thought because he would argue against their viewpoints his entire life. Understanding them also gives us a specific context in which to see how deeply Arnold influenced his viewpoint.

IN CHAPTER TWO OF *Culture and Anarchy*, Arnold laments the Victorian "bondage to machinery" and explains that what specifically is reprehensible about it is "our present proneness to value machinery as an end in itself, without looking beyond it to the end for which alone, in truth, it is valuable." The "end" that is valuable, of course, is humanity's search for greater knowledge and greater truth. To create greater wealth and comfort for their own sake was a descent into vulgarity for Arnold. Humanity must have its needs met before it can concentrate on the higher and more noble project of spiritual growth; but some people, the "Philistines," had become so enraptured and mesmerized by securing needs that they had entirely forgotten about the higher goal.

On this point Arnold agreed with his American contemporary, Henry David Thoreau, who used the analogy of a growing plant, explaining that when a seed is planted it must first establish roots but that once roots are created it begins its true journey, breaking the soil and reaching for the sun. In *Walden*, in the chapter titled "Economy," Thoreau laments that many of his townsfolk were so busy securing better and more comfortable "roots" that they never bothered to flower. Arnold also believed that this was exactly the problem. And good art and culture could supply the corrective because only the "want of light" had prevented people from looking "beyond machinery to the end for which machinery is valuable."[4]

Though Huxley had a somewhat different taste in art, a different esthetic of what is "sweet" and what is "light," he was in general agreement with Arnold about the illness and its cure. He, too, complained that society, in its view of industry and technology, had confused the means for the end—often citing, throughout his life, the biblical passage: "The Sabbath is made for man, and not man for the Sabbath," to make his point. Furthermore, because Huxley lived in the age of industry and technology, he considered it his duty as a literary man to discuss its specific issues. To those who night advise that he stick to his books and leave technology to the "experts," he explained:

> I feel strongly that the man of letters should be intensely aware of the problems which surround him, of which technological and scientific problems are the most urgent. It is his business to communicate his awareness and concern. Literature sets up a vision of man which guides people to a better understanding of themselves and their world.[5]

Conversely, when he was engaged in what seemed to be exclusively esthetic pursuits, Huxley asserted that he was not ignoring more current, pressing, or "practical" concerns, but only gathering sweetness and light with which to address them. In his introduction to *Texts and Pretexts*, his anthology of poetry published in 1933 during the Great Depression, Huxley explained:

> An anthology compiled in mid-slump? Fiddling, you protest indignantly, while Rome burns. But perhaps Rome would not now be burning if the Romans had taken a more intelligent interest in their fiddlers.
>
> We tend to think and feel in terms of the art we like; and if the art we like is bad, then our thinking and feeling will be bad. And if the thinking and feeling of most of the individuals composing a society is bad, is not the society in danger? To sit on committees and discuss the gold standard are doubtless public-spirited actions. But not the only public-spirited actions. They also serve who only bother their heads about art.

Huxley might have said "*especially* those who bother their heads about art" and, for him, this was especially true because so few people seemed to be bothering their heads about it at all. Society, in fact, was riding its technology toward abject ruin. The search for truth and beauty was being drowned out in the hum of the machine. And the seeker of beauty and truth was being dismissed by the "practical" man—the worker and the engineer. Huxley argued against three types of characters that he believed were growing increasingly prevalent in society and contributing to the "hum of the machine," each a victim for him of "Ford's disease."

The first character that he discredits is the overly industrious entrepreneur, typified for him by Ben Franklin, who constantly believes that only making money constitutes a practical life. Huxley, perhaps based on Max Weber's famous analysis, credits the Puritan theologian John Calvin with creating this absurd equation, the idea that the successful businessman is on a par, in terms of merit and value, with the philosopher or the artist.

A second type of character that irked Huxley his whole life was the sensualist, the "Good Timer," as he called it, and especially the man of means who lives only for pleasure and distraction. In *Do What You Will* he argues strongly against the search for incessant fun, saying that when he is exposed to it he can feel himself "sinking into deeper and deeper despondency." His first biographer, Bedford, explains that Huxley was opposed to those who constantly went to "grand restaurants," and we already know of his distaste for wanton promiscuity, which he argued, "spends itself purposelessly, without producing love, or even, in the long-run, amusement." In fact, Huxley believed that hedonism of any kind could never really satisfy the human mind, and so the hedonist is forced to search more and more frantically for larger and grander entertainments. Huxley found this not only vulgar but somehow pathetic. In the self-imposed death-in-life sentence of Myra Vivesh from *Antic Hay*, she has a cab driver take her and Theodore Gumbril (another "rabbit before a weasel") through Piccadilly over and over again, so she can see the bright lights.

> "Adorable lights!" said Mrs. Vivesh, as they drove once more through Piccadilly Circus.
>
> Gumbril said nothing. He had said all that he had to say last time.
>
> "And there's another," exclaimed Mrs. Vivesh, as they passed near Burlington House, a fountain of

Sandeman's port. "If only they had an automatic jazz band attached to the same mechanism!" she said regretfully.

The third character type most often criticized by Huxley is the busy-beaver, the clerk or factory worker who loses himself in hard work as a distraction he thinks noble in and of itself. And here we find Huxley in agreement with Lawrence who believed that "men that sit in machines, among spinning wheels, in an apotheosis of wheels" often become machines themselves. Huxley later explained that Lawrence often remarked that work could be a "stupefacient, like opium." Lawrence thought it immoral and once remarked to Huxley, "Think of the rest and peace, the positive sloth and luxury of idleness that work is." Work, Huxley and Lawrence believed, can cause us to shirk our first duty to life, which is to live.

Of course, many people, especially in the lower classes, must work, and Huxley was well aware of this fact. But for him this made their leisure time especially important, for it was only then that they were free to edify themselves and to free their minds. So much more to his distaste was the fact that the general public seemed mostly interested in superficial and passive pastimes, the "effortless pleasures," of listening to the radio, going to the cinema, and watching professional sports. He disliked jazz, at least the popular variety on the radio, with all its "brassy guffaw and caterwauling sentiment." Nor did he care for the superficiality and empty titillation of most movies. He equally disliked newspaper sensationalism, which was generally his complaint against the "yellow press"—that branch of the publishing industry (printed on cheap paper that quickly turned yellow and so displayed its intended obsolescence) that flooded the market with literary distractions. "That writing," he explained in "Writers and Readers," that "is not even intended to have a positive effect upon the reader—all that doughy, woolly, anodyne writing that exists merely to fill a gap of leisure, to kill time and prevent thought, to deaden and diffuse emotion."

Huxley wished people would become active and play sports rather than merely watch them. These pastimes, like work, were merely distractions, the watered-down pleasures of the wealthy "Good Timer." Admittedly they brought entertainment but, for Huxley at least, they brought little else. They created for the worker the illusion that the goal of work, the purpose of leisure, is pleasure and pleasure only. As early as his first book of essays he had argued against this:

> Of all the various poisons which modern civilization, by a process of auto-intoxication, brews quietly up within its own bowels, few, it seems to me, are more deadly (while none appears more harmless) than that curious and appalling thing that is technically known as "pleasure."

However, the workers, and especially the lower-class workers, were, for Huxley, to be somewhat forgiven their tendency to chase after pleasures because they were so relentlessly coerced and cajoled toward them by the incessant and manipulative advertising of the entrepreneurs. Capitalists were not only controlling their workers at work but also at play, fashioning "ready-made distractions" that robbed them of personal initiative and chances for creative outlet, even at home. Huxley explained in "The Victory of Art over Humanity," a little known essay from 1931 that David Bradshaw republished in his book *Aldous Huxley Between the Wars:*

> Our leisures are now as highly mechanized as our labors. . . the sphere of play no less than in that of work, creation has become the privilege of a fortunate few. The common man has always had to suffer from lack of money: he is now condemned to psychological poverty as well.

Claiming that this removal of creativity was not only pernicious but intended, Huxley in this same essay, openly criticized Henry Ford specifically for this condition. Ford, one of the richest men in the world, and perhaps *the* richest, was the most prominent figurehead of the mass production era and so an obvious target for Huxley. However, Huxley addressed him specifically because Ford had indeed said in his 1921 autobiography, *My Life and Work*, that mass production was helped along by the fact that some people have no use for creativity and don't enjoy it: "I could not possibly do the same thing day in and day out, but to other minds, perhaps I might say to the majority of minds, repetitive operations hold no terrors. . . To them the ideal job is one where the creative instinct need not be expressed."

Huxley was certainly aware of Ford's autobiography and detested his viewpoint, believing that it was propaganda for putting things the back way round. Train people not to think creatively, to take orders, and they become a more bovine work force. "Consolingly, Mr. Ford assures them that creation is a burden—a burden which, with Christ-like unselfishness, he offers to bear for them."[6]

Workers were selling their souls for just enough money to keep going and indulge in ready-made pleasures. They were being given, as Huxley often pointed out, "Bread and Circuses"—as were the Romans at the end of their civilization. And in this Huxley saw a lesson: that placating the working class was a much more effective tool for controlling them than using brute force. The capitalist likes a happy and fattened worker/consumer; but what was to happen to humankind if all of these vulgar character types continued to grow? What if everybody fell into torpor and mistook pleasure and comfort for the goal of human existence? In his 1927 essay "Comfort" from *Essays Old and New*, he warns:

> Comfort is a means not an ends. The modern world seems to regard it as an end in itself, an absolute good. One day, perhaps, the earth will have been turned into one vast feather-bed, with man's body dozing on top of it and his mind underneath, like Desdemona, smothered.

Huxley was happy that he was not being asked to participate, that he could think his own thoughts and bear up against the constant hum of machines and the constant whine of advertising proffering temptations he thought were destructive. Thank goodness the freedom to seek truth and light was not against the law. That personal choice, though not without conditioning to move away from it, existed. But what if it didn't? What if economic and political power were consolidated to a point of absolute control? And what if those who had control made pleasure and comfort the be all and end all of human existence? What if they used superior technology to intensify and proliferate those pleasures and comforts? The scenario of these possibilities became his fifth novel, *Brave New World*.

Published in 1931, *Brave New World* was as Jocelyn Brooke has observed, Huxley's "nearest approach to popular fiction." But the book seems to have had its genesis with an idea of pulling the leg of the famous author, H.G. Wells. Wells, a close friend of Julian and more than an acquaintance of Aldous, was then the most respected of the scientific popularizers advocating a bright future through technological progress. In 1923 Wells wrote *Men Like Gods* in which he outlined a scientifically created utopia based on socialism, secularism, state-controlled education, genetic engineering, and birth control. Huxley thought it might be interesting to use many of the same technologies and institutions to describe a dystopia, a negative utopia. Utopia literally means "no place." Wells was wistful that his paradise didn't yet exist, but Huxley would make one that Wells would be glad didn't.

Just two years before *Brave New World*, Huxley had written, in "Spinoza's Worm," some words that would prove ironically prophetic:

> My own feeling, whenever I see a book about the Future, is one of boredom and exasperation. What on earth is the point of troubling one's head with speculations about what men may, but almost certainly will not, be like in A.D. 20,000?[7]

Ten years earlier, in *Crome Yellow*, Huxley had had a character speculate that in the future, "in vast state incubators, rows upon rows of gravid bottles will supply the world with the population it requires. The family system will disappear . ." But in the late twenties, when

Huxley made his comment about the futility of writing about the future, he had been in his Lawrence phase and wishing people would settle down into the real world—which is always the present world. Two years later he seems to have found a reason for trying his hand at prophecy. Huxley hoped to create a satire of his own times that could act as a cautionary tale pointing up the tendency toward wholesale vulgarity. After his visit to the States in 1926 he wrote in *Proper Studies* that in America it seemed "all the resources of science are applied in order that imbecility may flourish and vulgarity cover the whole earth."[8] Now he would warn about that danger.

ROBERT S. BAKER, IN 1982, summarized Huxley's new society in *The Dark Historic Page*: "The World State is a wholly secular culture, dominated by economics, supported by technology, and dedicated to the—within carefully set limits—Freudian pleasure principle with its emphasis on libidinal appetites."[9]

Huxley begins his novel in the "Central London Hatchery and Conditioning Centre." On the front of the center's building is a shield that reads "Community, Identity, Stability"—the motto of the World State. Inside are row upon row of specially lined bottles in which human beings are grown eugenically. Later in the book we hear a line from a child's nursery rhyme: "Bye Baby Banting, Soon you'll need decanting." Huxley has the Hatchery Director sum up the process as "the principle of mass production at last applied to biology."

The citizens of the World State are all test-tube babies, created through "ectogenesis" (birthed externally) rather than "endogenesis" (birthed from inside of a woman), but the citizens are not all created equal. Some are tampered with intentionally while still in the bottle to create an inferior caste of beings (in fact, three inferior castes: the Gammas, Deltas, and Epsilons) to do menial work for the upper castes, the Alphas and Betas. As Henry Ford had said, not everyone wants to do scut work, so Huxley had the World State engineer castes of people who would. Mustapha Mond, one of the ten World Controllers, explains that ideally society "is modeled on the iceberg—eight-ninths below the water line, one-ninth above." And at the tippy top of the iceberg are the Controllers themselves, whose authority is absolute.

Mond is called "Your Fordship," instead of "Your Lordship," because in the World State Henry Ford is the prophet, and his auto-biography is their Bible. The novel takes place in the year 632 A.F., that is, six hundred thirty-two years after Ford invented the Model T. Soon after the Controllers take charge they cut the tops off all the crucifixes, making them into Ts, the sacred symbol. Here Huxley was having a bit of fun, but it is no coincidence that he was still singling Ford out personally as the apostle of his dystopia. He agreed with J.F.C. Fuller, a critic of Ford's, who wrote: "Not only is the Ford car produced in its millions, but also the Ford mind."[10] Moreover, he accused Ford of denigrating the arts—though here he is only accus-ing Ford of what Ford had already accused himself. Ford was openly and avowedly anti-art and anti-intellectual, famous for once saying, "history is bunk." But, as Fuller explained, Ford went even further: "Not only is history 'bunk' for Ford, but painting, sculpture, music, and all culture are bunk." "I don't like to read books," Ford once confessed, "they mess up my mind." It was for Henry's rage against Arnold's "light" that Huxley singled him out as the messiah of com-fort, convenience, and torpor.

Everyone in the World State, regardless of caste, is trained for only two things: work and pleasure. With the techniques of "neo-Pavlovian conditioning" and "hypnopaedia" (sleep-teaching) they are drilled from birth to be proud of their respective castes, as well as their respective jobs and pleasures. Children play "Centrafugal Bum-ble-puppy" and adults play "Electro-magnetic Golf." In addition to games there is something similar to a record player that emanates symphonies of odor, the "scent organ," and there are movies that include tactile sensations, the "feelies." But above and beyond these diversions, there is of course "soma," Huxley's name, borrowed from the ancient Aryan culture of India, for a strong intoxicant that is made available to everyone. Soma not only entertains, it helps one cope with and overcome one's worries. Huxley agreed with Karl Marx on the point that religion is very often a means of placating fear and worry, but why accept the "opiate of the masses" if there's an actual opiate that works better? Controller Mond explains that soma has "all the advantages of Christianity and alcohol; none of their defects."

But the gayest diversion—or, one should say, goal—for the adults of the World State is engaging in lots of sex with lots of partners. Lasciviousness is, in fact, the norm.

> "He patted me on the behind this afternoon," said Lenina.
> "There you see!" Fanny was triumphant. "That shows what he stands for. The strictest conventionality."

In the World State children are encouraged to play sex games from a very early age, and adults are punished for not staying properly infantile and promiscuous. When the Director of Hatcheries learns that one of his workers is not having regular sex, he reprimands him promptly: "If ever I hear again of any lapse from a proper standard of infantile decorum, I shall ask for your transference to a Sub-Centre—preferably to Iceland." Sex of the infantile variety is the wonderful goal, and in deference to Freud's belief that comfort and pleasure comprise the total needs of humanity, sometimes citizens of the World State use "O.F." to stand for "Our Freud" as well as "Our Ford." Huxley was often critical of Freud, preferring instead the psychological model of Carl Jung, who maintained that love and self-actualization are also fundamental human needs, like sex, food, and shelter.

If one is not in the mood for sex in this brave new world, there is always an ample supply of "sex hormone chewing gum" to stimulate the libido, so that in the end everyone is constantly seeking new partners. Sex, like soma, is just another drug for drowning the mind in pleasure—a comparison that Huxley has Lenina illustrate by singing in the shower. As she soaps up she chirps a popular tune, excitedly anticipating an upcoming date: "Hug me till you drug me, honey; Kiss me till I'm in a coma: Hug me, honey, struggly bunny; Love's as good as soma." (It's possible Huxley was trying his hand at writing a radio jingle with this little tune.)

In the world of comfort and pleasure that Huxley had created in *Brave New World* nothing else is of consequence. (When Bernard Marx, a psychologist and one of the main characters, complains to Lenina that he doesn't want to play Electro-magnetic Golf because he finds it a waste of time, Lenina asks "in some astonishment," "Then what's time for?") But into this world comes a savage (soon to he called, ironically, "Mr. Savage"), whose name is John. John, a Caucasian, was raised outside the World State among the barbarians of a New Mexico Indian reservation. Intrigued at first by his visit to the World State, he rapidly finds himself unable to adjust to its ethos of constant pleasure. He wants solitude to think his own thoughts and he wants love, specifically a special relationship with Lenina—but both solitude and emotional closeness are strictly forbidden by the Controllers. A herd mentality is preferred and maintained by regular "Solidarity Services" and sleep conditioning of the young. In youth they are given "at least a quarter of a million warnings against solitude."

But it isn't solitude or love for their own sake that motivate the "savage." While on the reservation he had found a copy of the complete works of Shakespeare, works which are forbidden in the World State but have become dear to John. In Huxley's *Brave New World*, John and, through him, Shakespeare, becomes the symbol of the search for sweetness and light, for truth and meaning. In chapter seventeen John is brought before Mond, an ironic fellow who knows that his society has traded truth for pleasure and comfort for meaning and who defends that position. When the savage complains about the superficiality of the World State's pastimes he gets into an argument with Mond about Shakespeare:

> "All the same," he insisted obstinately, "Othello's good, Othello's better than those feelies."
>
> "Of course it is," the Controller agreed. "But that's the price we have to pay for stability. You've got to choose between happiness and what people used to call high art. We've sacrificed the high art.

We have the feelies and the scent organ instead."

"But they don't mean anything."

"They mean themselves; they mean a lot of agreeable sensations to the audience."

Here Huxley, as has often been pointed out, is consciously paralleling the conversation between Jesus and the "Grand Inquisitor" in Dostoevski's *Brothers Karamazov*[11] Dostoevski has one brother telling another a parable about Jesus coming back to earth to lead his flock, only to be imprisoned by the priests of the Catholic Church. When Jesus is visited by the Inquisitor he is told that his rabble-rousing cannot be tolerated, and that his presence in the flesh would cause too much pain and political instability to be allowed. Better for everyone, and especially for those in control, to keep the flock under the protection of the Church. The Inquisitor continues: "With us all will be happy and will no more rebel nor destroy one another as under Thy freedom. Oh, we shall persuade them that they will become free when they renounce their freedom to us and submit to us."

Mond had also succeeded in keeping Jesus, along with truth and meaning, away from the masses. And to remind the reader of the present, Huxley has Mond tell the savage, delightedly: "Our Ford himself did a great deal to shift the emphasis from truth and beauty to comfort and happiness."

But agreeable sensations and stability are not enough for John and he engages Mond in further argument:

"But I don't want comfort. I want God, I want poetry, I want real danger, I want freedom, I want goodness, I want sin."

"In fact," said Mustapha Mond, "you're claiming the right to be unhappy."

"All right then," said the Savage defiantly, "I'm claiming the right to be unhappy."

And unhappy he becomes. Unable to escape the World State and his position as a comical celebrity, who does the most wonderfully absurd things, John is soon driven to hang himself, and so the novel ends.


BRAVE NEW WORLD WAS a major success for Huxley, with first year sales in Britain reaching 23,000 copies, and it remains the most popular of all his books. Today it is basic reading in high schools and colleges in the United States, but it was initially disliked in America and dismissed for being too pessimistic. H.G. Wells shared this sentiment, once writing to a friend about Huxley's "treason to science and defeatist pessimism," and in *The Shape of Things to Come* Wells dismissed Aldous's views as "alarmist fantasy." But *Brave New World* was not the first literary piece to suggest that science might bring a dark future. In fact, E.M. Forster had written his excellent short story, "The Machine Stops," even before the First World War. But *Brave New World* had become the most widely read, and critic George Kateb has speculated that it was the "most influential anti-utopian novel of the twentieth century" because it showed, chillingly, the most possible direction of things. Unlike George Orwell's *1984*, written seventeen years later, people of the industrialized West are today much more often bludgeoned with rhetoric and advertising than with clubs and brass knuckles. "In the end," said Mond, "the Controllers realized that force was no good. The slower but infinitely surer methods of ecogenesis, neo-Pavlovian conditioning and hypnopaedia" worked much better.

George Orwell (the pen name of Eric Blair) was, while a student at Eton, once a student of the young Aldous Huxley, but how different their opinions on how to control society. What they did share in common, however, was their fear about the loss of individuality and the loss of personal freedom. This is a main point in both their books and very significant for understanding Huxley's mind at the time. *Brave New World* ends bitterly, the "savage" having had made no change in the World State. In this regard the book continued Huxley's reputation as a cynic and pessimist. However, those who viewed him as only a cynic were clearly only reading his novels. In his books of essays Huxley was constantly suggesting a direction toward meaning and morality. In fact, later Huxley would give his own definition of cynicism to show that he did not fit it:

> Cynicism is the acceptance of things as they are, combined with the derisive knowledge that they couldn't he worse—a knowledge that is felt by the person who possesses it to excuse him from making any personal effort to change the intolerable situation.

Huxley was trying to change things—even early on, as his essays attest.

By the end of the twenties and in the early thirties it seems to have been his position that if he couldn't do it by writing the kind of transcendent, truth-generating novels he would have liked to write, then he would do it through essays. First he would argue for personal freedom—for in the individual act of reflection is the unit of a worthwhile society. Each citizen must contribute to the uplifting of society, and so the herd mentality is implicitly wrong. "In his philosophy of society," says Grover Smith, the compiler of Huxley's letters, "he stood with Jefferson. Whatever impinged upon human uniqueness, such as an ideology, political or religious, that won allegiance at the cost of individual function and experience . . would provoke his antipathies."[12]

Civilization couldn't call itself civilized for Huxley until it stopped its headlong movement away from individuality. Creating the World State of *Brave New World* could not be considered progress. It would be better to side with John the Savage and die. Primitives were preferable to robots, or as Huxley himself once explained, "Primitives are men who have never succumbed to the suicidal ambition to resemble ants."

His other and more important purpose in his essays of this time was to steer people toward the good books, and toward the good art, and then coach them to accept these. Art is a cure, and so Rome must pay attention to its fiddlers. Like Arnold, he believed it should be taken like a tonic. In *Music at Night* he tells us that "when art is best, beauty is truth." And later, in *Themes and Variations*, he equates the aesthetic experience with the mystical experience because it brings with it "insight as well as rapture." This is why literary criticism was so important to Huxley, as it was for Matthew Arnold, and not only literary criticism but analyses of all the arts. As Jacob Zeitlin, a friend of Huxley's, once pointed out, "The arts were not separate entities in his considerations. They were the intertwined expressions of the spirit and history of man." Huxley believed that sweetness and light were apprehensible through all the arts, and it's interesting to note here that the critical bibliography of his work lists forty-two essays on visual art alone.

What Huxley appreciated most was art that presented all of life. In *Do What You Will*, *Music at Night*, *The Olive Tree*, and *Themes and Variations* he gives us his criticism of the arts, and in *Texts and Pretexts* he gives us his recommendations of poetry. He had a lifelong fondness for Chaucer, who he argued accepted the crudities of life and its paradoxes without complaint and without a need to escape them. Huxley saw human beings as "multiple amphibians" and believed that art should present all aspects of their natures. In the visual arts he embraced Goya, El Greco, and Breugel the Elder for painting all of life, rather than hiding or sweeping under the carpet the mundane concerns of living—which, after all, take up most of our time. He praised Homer and Henry Fielding for these same virtues and explained that this rule of measure, which was certainly partially inspired by Lawrence, is the central concept of his criticism.

Of course, this is not to suggest that Huxley believed that depicting bodily functions necessarily made good art. More comprehensively he was arguing that since, as he put it, each human being is really a "colony of separate individuals," living in a variety of universes (mental, emotional, physical, etc.), art must call to all these aspects and stay true to them. If it did, or when it does, art has the ability to reorder inner space, to inspire the human being in all its dimensions, in the positive direction, away from decadence and vulgarity. In *Music at Night,* while specifically addressing the growing tendency toward empty sex, he gives us his general prescription for the plight of his generation: "Only a new mythology of nature, such as, in modern times, Blake, Robert Burns, and Lawrence have defined it, an untranscendental and (relatively speaking) realistic mythology of Energy, Life and Human Personality; will provide, it seems to me, the inward resistances necessary to turn sexual impulse into love, and provide them in a form which the critical intelligence of Post-Nietzschean youth can respect."[13]

In reading Huxley's materials from this period it is also clear that he was questioning whether there wasn't a more direct way to the wellspring of sweetness and light. He was still looking somehow to get beyond the door, to get beyond art, to the wellspring of art itself. To become fully an artist he believed he would first have to become fully himself. He was using art itself to find his way to this inner wellspring (during this period he reread Tolstoy's *War and Peace*, which he said was "a great consolation and a tonic") but he also wondered if there were other paths to it, and he was curious about the nature of sweetness and light itself. He wasn't sure what it was he was after but he sensed it—just as did Helmholtz Watson, the propagandist writer in *Brave New World*, who felt, "Really, and at the bottom, he was interested in something else. But in what? In what?"

Aldous Huxley in the 1920s

(Corbis Collection)

# - 6 -

# COMING TO AMERICA

*It's a rummy country, this. Just how rummy one can't tell*
*until one has driven about it in a Ford.*
—Aldous in a letter to his brother Julian

AFTER FINISHING *Brave New World* Huxley settled back into his life at Sanary. The summer of 1932 found the Huxleys basking in the Mediterranean sunshine and enjoying picnics with their friends, including the American novelist Edith Wharton and the French symbolist poet Paul Valery. Huxley also returned to working on his paintings, often having one member of the household pose while another read books aloud. "Really, it is the ideal art," he wrote in a letter in 1933, "involving one in nothing outside itself and having a technique which it is a pleasure to employ (when one thinks of the horror of using a pen or a typewriter!)." Huxley was particularly engrossed with issues of color and composition. He favored traditional themes and approaches, and would remain suspect of modern art all his life. In his novels we often find him lampooning one new style or another. In *Crome Yellow*, Mary, wishing to impress a young man, an artist, reveals her savvy of abstract art: "When I was in Paris this spring I saw a lot of Tschuplitski. . . . He's getting more and more abstract every day. He'd quite given up the third dimension when I was there and was just thinking of giving up the second. Soon, he says, there'll be just the blank canvas. That's the logical conclusion. Complete abstraction."

Huxley was enjoying himself that summer at Sanary, but he

couldn't stay long in the realm of the life-worshipper or the pure esthete before his own nature called him back to reflect on and explain
it. That fall he began to compile an anthology of poetry with commentaries called *Texts and Pretexts*. The "high art" that Mustapha
Mond and the other World Controllers of *Brave New World* would
wish to banish, Huxley was arguing must be embraced as a means of
lifting humanity up from meaninglessness and vulgarity.

In Huxley's efforts to explain the value of art and make specific
recommendations, it's interesting to note that where he had once
argued strongly against philosophy, he was now moving toward it.
Huxley was pondering the nature and value of art—that branch of
philosophy known as esthetics. Furthermore, since he maintained
that art's core purpose lies in its influence on morality, his esthetics
were intimately tied to ethics— yet another branch of philosophy. As
he articulated his various theories, Huxley came to realize that he was
slowly working out the details of a comprehensive worldview. On
some level this activity was certainly a sort of hypocrisy—in fact, the
very kind that Lawrence had accused him of. But it wasn't as much of
a compromise as it might at first appear.

Huxley still held that ultimate truth is experiential in nature and,
contrary to most Western philosophical traditions, cannot be known
through a collection of rational facts. However, to say that ultimate
truth is experiential does not mean that it can't be made sense of or
rationally explained. Huxley believed that it could and should be. For
though the intellectual analogue would be inferior to the truth (differ-
ing from it as a cake recipe differs from a cake), a philosophical description could have value if it led the intellect to accept the need to
transcend itself—to go beyond the ideas to the experiential truth itself.

Lawrence, of course, would not have agreed. It was his contention that, inevitably, people tend to mistake the description of the
thing for the thing itself—confusing a means for an ends—and wind
up in a dogmatic application of ideas. The history of religion and philosophy had proven this. "Whoring after abstractions" is only a way
of placating our discomfort with the wildness and complexity of the
universe. Abstractions encourage us to live in our heads instead of

our bodies. Huxley agreed with Lawrence on this point, but he also believed that, in the final analysis, the advantages of a good explanation outweighed the dangers. Huxley understood that human beings, consciously or unconsciously, embrace various viewpoints, cultural and personal, and on the basis of those viewpoints they find and dispense meaning—thereby constructing a philosophy. Because their culturally predisposed values feel so inherent and natural they may not realize that they are embracing a philosophy; nevertheless, Huxley recognized that they were. (Or to put it another way: They may believe themselves not to have a philosophy, not realizing it only looks that way from inside *their* philosophy.)

> To the "practical man" they [philosophical questions] may seem irrelevant. But in fact they are not. It is in the light of our beliefs about the ultimate nature of reality that we formulate our conceptions of right and wrong; and it is in the light of our conceptions of right and wrong that we frame our conduct, not only in the relations of private life, but also in the sphere of politics and economics. So far from being irrelevant, our metaphysical beliefs are the finally determining factor in all our actions.[1]

Huxley's philosophical thinking wasn't so much at odds with what he had earlier believed, as it was adding to it—a pattern he would generally follow throughout his life. As Sybille Bedford has described it, "Aldous did not so much change—he went on."[2] Humans create worldviews as spiders create webs, by nature, and then they reside in them as though those webs were given rather than created. They mistake artificial and analogical worlds for the real one; they misconstrue cultural or personal values for instinctual truth. This being the case, why not, with the proper warnings, create an analogue that points beyond analogues? That offers an antidote to "Jesus and Newton and Henry Ford's disease?"

Huxley's interest in creating a new set of first principles to justify the importance of art, the necessity of ethical behavior, and the experiential nature of truth intensified during the summer of 1933. The previous January Adolph Hitler had become chancellor of Germany. In February he had used a fire in the German Parliament as an excuse to close the government and set up a police state, effectively ending the constitution of the Weimar Republic. Many writers and artists had fled, either because they were in danger of arrest or for reasons of conscience, fearing the growing conservatism and censorship. Many, especially in the second group, came to Sanary, and they brought with them their fears of another war. Aldous and Maria had left Italy when the fascists had started opening their mail and disapproving of their ideas; they had moved to Sanary to get away from fascism and politics. But now Thomas Mann, Bertolt Brecht, and other writers with whom they were socializing pulled them back into an awareness of what was going on. Huxley's sense of moral duty awakened, and he reasoned that if there was ever a time to point out a higher meaning and purpose, it was then.

That year, 1934, Aldous published, in addition to *Texts and Pretexts* and the collected letters of D.H. Lawrence, a travelogue of a trip that he and Maria had taken to the Caribbean, Mexico, and Central America, entitled *Beyond the Mexique Bay*. But he had not published a novel in two years and was not to publish another one for two more. (He had started a novel two years before, and it had gone well at first, but then it stalled.) His novels paid better than travelogues or books of essays, and Huxley still wished to have his artistic breakthrough, but his muse was not obeying him.

That winter the Huxleys moved to London to be closer to family and friends (though Aldous's father, Leonard, had died the year before) and took a seven-year lease on an apartment in the fashionable Albany district, near Piccadilly. They would return to Sanary for the summers but hoped that the intellectual climate of London would jump-start Aldous's muse. This was not to be. The cramped quarters of their apartment, the poor light, and the cold weather of the London winter, along with fears about a possible war, conspired to keep Aldous from bringing his stalled novel to completion. Instead he felt frustrated and depressed, and was suffering from various ailments, including insomnia.

Huxley's main support during this difficult period, beyond his wife and son (Matthew, with whom Aldous was never a doting father, was then a teenager at Dartington School) came from another writer with whom he'd worked on the short-lived journal, *The Realist*. His name was Gerald Heard and the two had met through a mutual friend, Raymond Mortimer, in 1929. After 1934 Heard and Huxley became not only close but nearly inseparable. Aldous had found not only a new primary friendship, after the one with Lawrence, but also a new primary influence—one he believed could help him uncover the first principles he so deeply believed were needed.

Heard, five years older than Huxley, had won undergraduate honors at Cambridge and then gone on to do graduate work in the philosophy of religion. He left college however, without finishing his graduate degree and went directly to publishing various theories on life and meaning that were generally well-respected in the intellectual community. In fact, it has been said that Heard is "one of the best kept secrets of the twentieth century."[3] Like Aldous, he had an encyclopedic memory and read broadly across the disciplines, bringing together in his work ideas from anthropology, sociology, history, religion, and the various sciences. He was a persuasive speaker with a charismatic personality and, perhaps encouraged by his homosexuality, he was also a liberal. Also like Huxley, he wished to be of some use to humanity, believing that whatever worldview one creates, it only has value if it helps humanity—once observing, "Cosmology must end in ethics."[4]

Heard was the extrovert of the two but his ideas excited demonstrative interest in Aldous and the two often sat up talking late into the night. Their friendship was the beginning of an alliance that would bear fruit for many years to come. During the next fifteen years their respective publications were often parallel reports of their collective conclusions. Comparing Huxley's *Ends and Means* with Heard's *The Third Morality* (both published in 1937) or Huxley's *The Perennial Philosophy* (1945) with Heard's *The Eternal Gospel* (1946) we see many close similarities. What Heard gave Huxley was a strong philosophical foundation for his growing theories about art and ethics, and what Huxley gave Heard were well-thought-out explanations of the present social and cultural circumstances. Both men were troubled about the condition of society and culture and both agreed that what was holding civilization back was the same set of causes that were leading to war. Though their explanations of why this was so differed, they soon realized that their views were compatible—even in a sense completed each other—and in long discussions they worked out the details of a synthesis.

Heard recommended that Aldous try meditation and yoga to help with his poor health and insomnia. He also introduced Huxley, in the fall of 1935, to Dr. F.M. Alexander, an Australian therapist whom Virginia Woolf's husband once called "a quack—but an honest and inspired quack." Huxley learned Alexander's technique of "kinesthetic re-education," which involved relearning how to walk, sit, lift objects, and generally move one's body. Alexander argued that most people have developed bad habits in the use of their bodies and these habits have led to a deterioration of their health. Since mind and body are strongly interrelated, the poor use of one adversely affects the other. He convinced Aldous (as well as John Dewey, George Bernard Shaw, and his other patients) that relearning how to use his body could alleviate his depression. Huxley's experiments with the Alexander technique reinforced that belief; he followed Alexander's advice and recommended it all his life. This recognition of the body's influence on the mind and the mind's influence on physical health and the body (which was also part and parcel of the theory behind his yoga and meditation practices) greatly impressed him. Not only was it holistic, something Huxley had always advocated, but it illustrated his belief in the viability of reeducation. "If reflexes can be conditioned, then obviously, they can be reconditioned." It was one proof that people *could* learn another way of living.

His time spent with therapists, practicing meditation and yoga, and talking all night with Heard, were in some ways distractions from finishing his novel but, interestingly enough, they also helped him finish it. Even as late as the fall of 1935 he wrote to his friend Robert Nichols, "Here I'm hard at work on a novel that won't get finished," but by the spring of 1936 it was wrapped up and titled *Eyeless in Gaza.* Using the philosophy he was putting together with Heard (which had been consuming his attention and brightening his mood), Huxley created chapters he then inserted throughout the novel.

These chapters, given as extracts from the diary of the main character, Anthony Beavis, describe not only Beavis's spiritual growth but Huxley's too. In the novel Huxley argues, in agreement with his discussions with Heard, that nations put too much attention on the state and too little on the individuals who make up the state—that nations should only matter in so much as they help individuals. Sacralizing the state is working from the top down instead of from the bottom up, and therefore creates a skewed view of truth and values.

> . . .think in terms of individual men, women, and children, not of States, Religions, Economic Systems and such-like abstractions:
> there is then a hope . . . For if you begin by considering concrete people, you see at once that freedom from coercion is a necessary condition of their developing into full-grown human beings; that the form of economic prosperity which consists in possessing unnecessary objects doesn't make for individual well-being; that a leisure filled with passive amusements is not a blessing; that the conveniences of urban life are bought at a high physiological and mental price . . . that a social organization resulting in individuals being forced, every few years, to go out and murder one another must be wrong. And so on. Whereas if you start from the State, the Faith, the Economic System, there is a complete transvaluation of values. Individuals must murder one another . . . must live in towns . . . must be encouraged to buy things they don't need, because the industrial system exists and has to be kept going; must be coerced and enslaved, because otherwise they might think for themselves and give trouble to their rulers[5]

Gerald Heard, 1948

(Vedanta Archives, Vedanta Society of Southern California)

Aldous Huxley
lecturing in 1963

(Collection of the
Los Angeles Public Library)

Both Huxley and Heard had increasingly come to believe that the most overlooked cure for social problems is actually the improvement of the individual citizen, and that cultures are only expressions of the collective consciousness of their people. Huxley wrote in *Eyeless in Gaza*, "Today's national behavior—a large-scale projection of today's individual behavior." And both men wondered what national behavior could be projected if people learned to meditate, do yoga, and try Alexander's techniques of physical reeducation. Certainly it would create a grassroots impetus toward positive change and a foundation for more humanistic programs at the macro level of society. "I've always felt," Aldous wrote to Julian, "that it was vitally necessary for people to have some efficient technique for personal development—for obviously sociological and mechanical improvements can't produce their best effects on people who are mentally and spiritually undeveloped and barbarous."[6]

Huxley and Heard reasoned that the unit of world peace is individual peace, that a forest is only as green as the individual trees in the forest are green; if the trees aren't green, the forest can't be green. Cultivate the individual and you spontaneously affect the foundation of society. But how do you bring the individual to peace?

In *Eyeless in Gaza*, Dr. Miller, a character based mainly on Heard (and, after Rampion, the second prophet of goodness in a Huxley novel) explains to Anthony Beavis that personal peace is gained through direct contact with the roots of consciousness, the "Divine Ground" of being and becoming. Here Huxley was outlining a viewpoint he had borrowed from Heard—a belief in a spiritual reality underlying the phenomenal world, a kind of "world soul." This viewpoint forms the foundation of Huxley's mature philosophy, which he later called the perennial philosophy.

HEARD HAD BEEN STUDYING mysticism since at least the mid-twenties, probably inheriting an interest in it from George Russell, the Irish mystic and poet, whom he had met while working as a secretary for Sir Horace Plunkett, a wealthy supporter of the Irish cultural renaissance. Heard's mysticism was somewhat eclectic but he mainly followed the Advaita (nondual) branch of Vedanta philosophy, an Indian viewpoint that had, more than a century earlier, influenced such German philosophers as Schelling and Schiller, and through them such others as Coleridge and Emerson. Advaita Vedanta, based mainly on the Upanishads, a group of Sanskrit texts composed between the eighth and third centuries, B.C., maintains that all of reality emerges from one infinite, unbounded source of spiritual energy called *Brahman*—capitalized here to signify its absoluteness. Of course, some of the "things" in creation are human beings—so we, too, are connected to Brahman, and in essence nondifferent from it. Brahman is, in fact, the essence of everything. It is at the heart of the atom and it is out beyond the rim of the universe—or as the famous Upanishadic axiom states, "I am That, you are That, all this is That, and That alone is."

Heard and Huxley had become very excited about the possible ramifications of this unifying principle. When the Hindu scripture states *Tat tvan asi,* "You are That," it is issuing us a wake-up call to stop thinking of ourselves as only physical beings muddling through the work-a-day world. In other words, we may think of ourselves as only a man or a woman, but in reality we are also the infinite, unchanging, timeless oneness of Brahman, an absolute field of pure energy and intelligence. Waves on the ocean, so the analogy goes (an analogy that Huxley would often use), are not ultimately individual entities; they are, at their source, the ocean itself. Unfortunately, we are prevented from realizing our "ocean" side, according to Vedantists, because without refinement of our consciousness, we mistake the realm of change and multiplicity, including our bodies and minds, as the whole story of existence.

This is lamentable, Huxley believed, because without knowing the experience of who we really are, we in some sense know nothing at all. The value of all knowledge and experience in life is relative to the knower and, to put it simply, without knowing who we really are, how can we know what we really like, want, or need? Without knowing itself as ocean, the wave lacks perspective and so flounders in its appreciation of life. "It is because we don't know who we are, because we are unaware that the Kingdom of Heaven is within us, that we behave in the generally silly, the often insane, the sometimes criminal ways that are so characteristically human."[7]

Huxley also found compelling the Vedantist's claim that truth is ultimately experiential—that realizing the state of mystical enlightenment (called *vidya, bodhi, jivanmukti,* etc.) was the ultimate goal. Truth can be described, but it is not ultimately an idea. It is a state of being, a condition of consciousness.

Huxley argued that happiness is dependent upon many variables, physical as well as spiritual, and in Vedanta he found a unifying concept for his philosophy. Earlier in his career he had rejected mysticism, often poking fun at it in his novels—for instance, when talking about Mr. Barbecue-Smith's book "Pipelines to the Infinite" in *Crome Yellow* or the phony palm-readings of Madam Sesostris (a name later borrowed by T.S. Eliot and used in *The Wasteland*). For a time, around 1925, Huxley's thinking about mysticism began to change somewhat as he flirted with Indian philosophy. We see the effects of this in *Those Barren Leaves*, when, at the end, he has Mr. Calamy turn to a life of spiritual contemplation to get "beyond the limitations of ordinary existence." However, two things still had discouraged him from mysticism: his trip to India later that year, the squalor of which convinced him that such views led to disinterest in practical life, and then his reunion with Lawrence, who thought mysticism a business of escapism, based mainly on an ascetic denial of the body.

But Heard was to change Huxley's discouragement, convincing him that mysticism could be practical; in fact, that it was *most* practical. By gaining an awareness of the "Divine Ground," the true self, the individual could permanently embrace "the peace of God that passeth all understanding"—could own the source and goal of Matthew Arnold's "sweetness and light." What art and poetry only gave glimpses of, mysticism could make a permanent resource. This last idea intrigued him immensely; for at that time he already was questioning the efficacy of literature and art for keeping humanity away, permanently, from vulgarity. Perhaps other means should be explored, too; means that could be even more effective. Very revealing of Huxley's thinking at the time is a passage from *Eyeless in Gaza:*

Mr. Croyland . . . went on. "The great artists carry you up to heaven."

"But they never allow you to stay there," Mark Staithes objected. "They give you just a taste of the next world, then let you fall back, flop, into the mud. Marvellous while it lasts. But the times's so short. And even while they've actually got me in heaven, I catch myself asking: Is that all? Isn't there anything more, anything further? The other world isn't other enough. Even Macbeth, even the Mass in D, even the El Greco Assumption." He shook his head. "They used to satisfy me. They used to be an escape and a support. But now . . . now I find myself wanting something more, something heavenlier . . ."

In Vedanta Huxley saw a possible means of reaching a higher heaven—and a heaven that was wonderfully non-different from this earth (as Lawrence argued it shouldn't be), requiring a shift in consciousness and perception rather than a relocation in space, or an escape from it.

IN THE FALL OF 1935, after the Italian fascists had invaded Ethiopia and war seemed more imminent, Huxley, armed with his new ideas, joined the Peace Pledge Union (PPU) of the Reverend H.R.L. Sheppard. Sheppard, a Canon of St. Paul's Cathedral and a Dean of Canterbury, was a well-loved clergyman who a year earlier had written an open letter to the press regarding the war. In the letter he asked that those who agreed with him that "war of every kind or for any cause, is not only a denial of Christianity, but a crime against humanity, which is no longer to be permitted by civilized people" send him a postcard. No cards came for two days, but on the third day the post office was filled with bags of mail addressed to Sheppard. The response amounted to more than a hundred thousand cards. This was the beginning of the PPU; Heard joined the movement in the early fall of 1935 at its start, and by December Huxley was also on stage as one of the keynote speakers advocating strict pacifism. At the root of Huxley's message, of course, was his belief that the unit of world peace is individual peace. "If enough people address themselves to living up to this belief, if enough people set out to experience [this] spiritual reality . . .then there will be peace; for peace . . . is a by-product of a certain way of life."

Society wasn't progressing, evolving; it was degenerating into a series of mob mentalities (fascism in Italy and Germany, and communism in Russia) that offered the individual a kind of solace but at too great a price. It gave them freedom from choosing rather than the freedom to choose. It was a wrong transcendence of the self, relieving the individual of responsibility but simultaneously empowering tyrants like Hitler, Mussolini and Stalin. And in England and America Huxley and Heard believed things weren't much better. Workers were placated with pleasures and comforts, while the capitalists who ruled them became increasingly wealthy and powerful. "Progress" had become the central tenet of culture but there was very little discussion of what the progress was aiming at. A particular kind of technological "feel good" change had become an end in itself. "One goes on believing in automatic progress, because one wants to cherish this stupidity: it's so consoling. Consoling, because it puts the whole responsibility for everything you do or fail to do on somebody or something other than yourself."[8]

In the current torpor, individuals were easily coerced into believing whatever fantasy the powers-that-be dictated. But if individuals could reeducate themselves to be more aware, to use meditation to contact the source of all awareness, the illusions would drop away and they would have a yardstick for measuring any new illusions they encountered. "The fundamental principle," Heard says in *The Third Morality,* "whereby the growing spirit knows all those things that should be avoided is this: whatsoever will keep the individual arrested in his individuality and incapable of growing into the enlarged life that lies ahead [in oneness with Brahman], that is deadly to life."

Huxley had found a philosophy in consonance with his various theories, one that fulfilled them and contradicted no scientific facts (an important point for Aldous). However, despite this watershed in his investigations, by the fall of 1936 things were not going well for him. *Eyeless in Gaza*, though as ambitious as *Point Counter Point*, had obtained mixed reviews, with some critics feeling that the book was too preachy, too sanctimonious—as if the tract had invaded the novel. It seemed that Huxley's credibility as a novelist depended upon his maintaining a strict cynicism. When he offered a prophet of hope such as Dr. Miller, or a convert from pessimism such as Anthony Beavis in *Eyeless in Gaza*, many critics were not willing to go along with him.

On top of this the PPU was losing steam as many who had sponsored it before changed their stripes in reaction to escalations in fascist aggression. (Germany had just given assistance to its fellow fascists in the Spanish Civil War.) And so when Huxley's pamphlet for the PPU, "What Are You Going to Do About It?" came out, Leonard Woolf argued against its blind idealism, and Cecil Day Lewis, in his article "We're Not Going To Do NOTHING" for *The Left Review*, said that England was not yet at the point where there was no recourse but to "while away the time with Mr. Huxley's spiritual exercises."

Huxley answered his accusers, arguing that a "99% pacifism" wouldn't work, that one couldn't be a pacifist and still select "the war that suits us," but he was getting tired of public life—and especially of being in the spotlight. On November 27 he gave his last lecture for the PPU, at Royal Albert Hall. The possibility of peace was quickly receding and Huxley also realized, intensely, that he didn't like being cast in the role of a leader or spokesman. He was, as he put it, "completely unsuited to political life," with "no power to organize things and very bad on committees." It best suited his personality to work behind the scenes, arguing a philosophical position while keeping a private life.

Back at Sanary after Christmas, Huxley began to write a book-length endorsement of pacifism, advocating methods for achieving it from every angle—economically, educationally, personally, socially, and politically. The book would contain references to the present situation but he hoped also to reveal the deeper psychological and sociological roots of war, which he had studied for years and which he now believed were intimately related to the spiritual poverty rampant in Western culture.

During the previous fall he and Heard had discussed the possibility of launching a lecture tour in the United States, where the pacifist movement was still quite strong and might be further strengthened. This would require more time onstage for Huxley, but during the winter Heard had persuaded him that the cause was good and the tour would be short. Heard, once a science reporter for the BBC, had also convinced the Huxleys that the new weapons developed in preparation for the war were so deadly that if war broke out it could mean the total devastation of Europe. Maria was especially worried by this idea and consequently discussed with Aldous the possibility of sending their son Matthew to college in America. The trip for the lecture tour would give the Huxleys a chance to check out schools—and perhaps they could visit Frieda Lawrence in New Mexico. The trip was planned and they hoped for a stay, according to one of Maria's letters, for "nine months or a year." What they did not anticipate were certain enticements that eventually would make their move permanent. The Huxleys had set off for a brief visit and remained living in America for the rest of their lives.

AT THE END OF FEBRUARY they left Sanary for good, putting the house up for sale and giving the Bugatti they had owned for many years to Renee Kisling, wife of the famous Polish painter Moise Kisling. On April 7, 1937, they sailed from Southampton on the *S.S. Normandie* with Gerald Heard and his sometimes lover, Chris Wood. The Huxleys had booked an inexpensive cabin to cut costs but when the French line learned who was aboard they insisted on putting them in better accommodations. Maria was surprised by the attention—and even more surprised once they reached New York, writing to one of her sisters, "You have no idea how famous Aldous is here," and adding, "perhaps I shall end by being impressed. Paramount newsreels came to shoot us."

After a brief visit to New York, hosted by Huxley's American publisher, Harper & Brothers, the Huxleys and Heard prepared to visit several universities to scout them for Matthew and for the peace tour. Among them was Duke University, where Huxley and Heard would give a lecture and look at the ESP laboratory of Dr. J.B. Rhine. Then they would go on to New Mexico and visit Frieda.

They bought a car big enough for the four of them and all their baggage. The car was a Ford—certainly a surprise, given Aldous's feelings about the company's owner, and a choice, unfortunately, about which he made no recorded comment. The trip took them five weeks and Maria did all the driving. They passed through Virginia, Georgia, Florida, Louisiana, and Texas on their way south and west. This was the time of the Great Depression, and the Huxleys were amazed at the widespread poverty they saw. As David King Dunaway has observed in *Huxley in Hollywood*, once they were in Texas they drove along the same dusty roads, at exactly the same time, and with the same types of people, as Steinbeck later portrayed in *The Grapes of Wrath*. Finally they arrived at San Cristobal, 8,000 feet above the valley of the Rio Grande, near Taos, New Mexico. Lawrence's homestead was fairly rustic, but quiet and pleasant, with spectacular views of the valley. "Freida is well, cheerful, and a great deal calmer than she used to be," Aldous wrote to Julian. "Later middle age is suiting her."

Soon after arriving Huxley set up shop in a small cabin and began finishing his comprehensive book on pacifism. He poured himself into the project. He had by then thought his thesis through and for the first time was comfortable with himself writing as a philosopher, an important transition in his development.

Sometime a year or two earlier he had read the studies of Dr. William Sheldon, a physician who maintained that there are three broad categories of human personality based upon three particular body types: the endomorph, the mesomorph, and the ectomorph. The endomorphic body type is soft and round and dominated by the digestive tract; the mesomorphic is athletic and dominated by the muscles; while the ectomorphic is thin-boned and thin in general. These body types give rise, according to Sheldon, to the *viscertonic* personality (comfort-loving and jovial), the *somatonic* (loving action and adventure), and the *cerebrotonic* (intellectual and inwardly focused).

Sheldon held that people are usually composites of the three types, though often more strongly one than another. Applying Sheldon's tests for determining type, Huxley found that he was almost purely a *cerebrotonic ectomorph,* a person constructed naturally to be thin and thoughtful.

Sheldon's work convinced Huxley that his intellectual nature was not so much a barrier to knowing his physical self as it was a projection of it. Sheldon's theories supported Huxley's belief that human nature is complex and multifaceted, while still allowing him to see his intellectuality as endemic to who he was. This was the beginning of Huxley's wholesale acceptance of himself as a philosopher, and *Ends and Means*, published in 1937, became his first book-length, systematic presentation of a philosophical position. In it he was specifically attempting to "relate the problems of domestic and international politics, of war and economics, of education, religion and ethics, to a theory of the ultimate nature of reality."

Huxley resisted the label of philosopher all his life, preferring instead to he called a "man of letters." The distinction is a matter of semantics; he disliked the label because it was generally used to define a person engaged in a particular, formal pursuit in which truth is believed to be discernible from the intellect. Huxley disagreed with this position. But from a broader perspective, in which philosophy is taken as the intellectual search for meaning, Huxley was, as many have later remarked, an important twentieth-century philosopher.

*Ends and Means* starts from the premise that only good means will bring good ends, and that good ends cannot justify bad means. But at the heart of his analysis, which runs to more than four hundred pages, is his belief in the primacy of cultivating the individual mind and heart. Huxley was convinced that there exists (or, at least, there *could* exist) a trans-rational, trans-cultural truth underlying the material universe. And since it was trans-cultural (dependent upon no humanly created values or ideals), it was also pan-cultural, available to everyone—and therefore a potential means of uniting human beings one to the other through their mutual essence. As all waves are a part of one ocean. Here Huxley was arguing in agreement with his character Anthony Beavis in his soliloquy at the end of *Eyeless in Gaza:* ". . united at the depths with other lives, with the rest of being. United in peace. . . . For beneath all being, beneath the countless identical but separate patterns, beneath the attractions and repulsions, lies peace. . . . Peace from pride and hatred and anger, peace from craving and aversions, peace from all the separating frenzies. . . Peace in the depths, under the storm, far down below the leaping of the waves, the frantically flying spray."[9]

If this sounded too good to be true, Huxley only asked that his readers consider his logic and explain where it failed. He wasn't advocating a return to supernaturalism. If anything, he was after an embrace of supra-naturalism, of a being and truth transcendental to the purely physical level of existence. Of course, since this being was, in essence and by nature, beyond relative physical existence, science could never verify it—in fact, could never either prove or disprove its existence. But this Being, this Brahman, would not contradict science, and that it couldn't be verified by science did not mean that it couldn't he experienced. In fact, Huxley believed the reality of this situation illustrated the limitations of science. In other words, because something can't he quantified doesn't prove it doesn't exist. Huxley noted that we must face the fact that science can only go so far, because if we don't, too much of the human experience will be sacrificed.

> Reality as actually experienced contains intuitions of
> value and significance, contains love, beauty, mysti-
> cal ecstasy, intimations of godhead. Science did not
> and still does not possess intellectual instruments
> with which to deal with these aspects of reality. . . .
> It is worthwhile to quote in this context the words
> with which Hume closes his *Enquiry.* "If we take in
> our hand any volume; of divinity or school meta-
> physics, for instance; let us ask, Does it contain any
> abstract reasoning concerning quantity or number?
> No. Does it contain any experimental reasoning
> concerning matter of fact or evidence? No. Commit
> it then to the flames; for it can contain nothing but

sophistry and illusion." Hume mentions only divinity and school metaphysics; but his argument would apply just as cogently to poetry, music, painting, sculpture, and all ethical and religious teaching. *Hamlet* contains no abstract reasoning concerning quantity or number and no experimental reason concerning evidence; nor does the Hammerklavier Sonata, nor Donatello's David, nor the *Tao Te Ching*, nor the *Following of Christ*. Commit them therefore to the flames: for they can contain nothing but sophistry and illusion.

We are living now, not in the delicious intoxication induced by the early successes of science, but in a rather grisly morning-after, when it has become apparent that what triumphant science has done hitherto is to improve the means for achieving unimproved or actually deteriorated ends. In this condition of apprehensive sobriety we are able to see that the contents of literature, art, music—even in some measure of divinity and school meta-physics— are not sophistry and illusion, but simply those elements of experience which scientists chose to leave out of account, for the good reason that they had no intellectual methods for dealing with them.[10]

Huxley advocated that whether Brahman exists or not should be found out through stringent effort to experience it, and that enlightenment as a possible phenomenon should not be dismissed out of hand. Scientists, he said, may disclaim mysticism as "subjective and illusory" but should remember that any direct intuition must seem subjective and illusory to those who haven't experienced it yet; for instance, that it is impossible for "the deaf to form any idea of the nature or significance of music." He suggested that his critics should be more empirical. He cast the ball back into their court, asking of the scientists the same open-mindedness his grandfather, Thomas Huxley, had once asked of the Church—to remember as they doubted, those "Pisan professors who denied, on *a priori* grounds, the validity of Galileo's direct intuition (made possible by the telescope) of the fact that Jupiter has several moons."

Whether or not one agrees with Huxley's conclusions, *Ends and Means* remains a brilliant, sustained argument in support of pacifism and for understanding Huxley, it is one of his most important books. When it was released, Huxley's picture filled the cover of the *New York Times Book Review* of December 12, 1937, but the review—like many others the book received—was mixed. Only a few critics seemed to grasp what Huxley was up to, and many intellectuals disregarded him. "Huxley's arguments," Dunaway sums up, "against capitalist greed, war, torture, and press censorship were casually ignored as if a novelist had no business commenting on such matters."[11] George Orwell, however, disagreed with the critics and offered a last word on Huxley's behalf: "Anyone who helps put peace on the map is doing useful work."

Huxley had thrown down his theory like an intellectual gauntlet, but now, whether people listened or not, he himself had to prove it. Unless he experienced enlightenment himself, he would have to remain somewhat skeptical of it. To further his experiment, he was deeply interested in contacting experts in the techniques of meditation and mystical awakening. Books weren't enough—and most books recommended finding a teacher, a spiritual guide, anyway. Huxley was curious to find out what a guru could do and if a guru was necessary. He would be a guinea pig, so to speak, for the enlightenment theory and the path to it. The question now was: where to find a teacher?

# - 7 -

# THE PERENNIAL PHILOSOPHY

*I wish I could see any remedy for the horrors*
*of human beings except religion or could see any religion*
*that we could all believe in.*
—Aldous Huxley

THE VEDANTA PHILOSOPHY PROVIDED Aldous with exciting explanations, but of course explanations do not constitute proof. Huxley wrote in *Ends and Means* that direct experience was needed, and so, "abstract reasoning must now give place." He threw himself into the task of finding methods for "establishing communion between the soul and the integrating principle of the universe." He and Heard set out to perform an enormous experiment of no fixed duration, a project that would certainly take years, and perhaps a lifetime—whatever its final conclusion. However, Huxley was not, in actuality or by inclination, ready to give up the world and become a monk. He wished to find a path that would allow him to remain in the world and allow him to work for peace and justice. Also, he had a wife and son to support; he needed money and would have to continue writing—especially since his novels at that point were selling at an all-time low.

While discussing what he might do to support his family after the peace tour with Gerald, Frieda suggested writing scripts for the movies. Her friend, Jacob Zeitlin, a rare book dealer in Los Angeles, had some contacts at the Hollywood studios, and she was sure he would be willing to act as an intermediary. This was, obviously, an odd proposition for Aldous. He had argued so often against the flicker-ing-feel-good of the cinema, but it could be lucrative, which was important now with Matthew about to start college. Then too, even if movies were generally inane that didn't mean they had to be. Several respected novelists, including William Faulkner and F. Scott Fitzgerald, were already in Hollywood attempting to do things properly. Why couldn't Huxley? Heard and Huxley were also both aware that California was home to a major branch of the Vedanta Society, an organization established by an Indian saint, Swami Vivekananda. The two men had more than a dilettante's interest in Vedanta; they hoped to learn its techniques of meditation, and they were curious to study the tradition with its actual representatives and experts.

Leaving Frieda's, the Huxleys and Heard went briefly to Hollywood to feel things out and establish a presence at the studios. They were still committed to their fall lecture tour of college campuses but hoped to line things up for script writing as well and, afterward, hoped to meet Swami Prabhavananda, the leader of the Hollywood Vedanta center. Huxley quickly worked up a scenario for a possible film and enlisted Anita Loos, author of *Gentlemen Prefer Blondes*, an acquaintance from his first U.S. visit in 1926, to help him shop it around at the studios. Nothing definite panned out, though there were possibilities; meanwhile, Huxley and Heard prepared to head off by train on their tour for pacifism. The peace movement was strong in the United States at the time and Heard and Huxley generally met large audiences and eager ears. Maria, who stayed behind in California (and eventually drove the Ford, alone, to New York to meet Aldous) had attended the first lecture in Los Angeles, and in a letter described the two men's styles of lecturing: "Aldous so slow and calm and passive, Gerald vehement and busy and coercive."

The tour was a success but Huxley again realized that he didn't like being in the spotlight. Not only because he didn't like public speaking but because he felt that much of what he said fell on deaf ears. His message from *Ends and Means*, which emphasized the importance of personal awakening—including the commitment to wake up that must be made by those in the audience—seemed to get lost in superficial talk about politics in Europe. Such superficiality dis-

couraged him and reinforced his tendency toward cynicism. He wrote
to his brother Julian from the tour:

> I find myself often a bit overwhelmed by the curious
> rigidity and opacity of most human beings. There's
> something dismally fixed, stony, sclerotic about
> most of them—a lack of sensibility and awareness
> and flexibility, which is most depressing. There
> seems to be nothing much to be done, beyond, of
> course, doing one's best to prevent the oncoming of
> mental sclerosis in oneself, to keep the mind open to
> the world and to that which transcends the world.[1]

After the tour ended, Aldous and Maria spent Christmas together
in Rhinebeck, New York, and then prepared to return to Europe.
Matthew would stay behind and go to school in Colorado. But at the
last minute, word reached Huxley that one of his script ideas had
been accepted by MGM, and they returned to Hollywood. As it
turned out, the idea was not accepted; instead the studio pitched
Aldous a job working on the script for a film about Madam Curie
starring Greta Garbo. The job paid well and Huxley was between
books, so he took it.

Once in California, they rented a small house in Beverly Hills.
Heard, who was already there visiting his friend Chris Wood, moved
in with the Huxleys, and Maria did the running around for both men.
She liked California's "Mediterranean ease" better than the East
Coast, where people were "more like the English and freezing," but
she sometimes grew weary of playing secretary, housekeeper, and
driver for someone else besides Aldous. Huxley couldn't drive because of his poor eyesight and Heard simply refused to learn. Consequently, Maria was constantly shuttling them places. When she regis-
tered at hotels during this period she would write under "profession,"
"chauffeur."

Aldous worked on "Madam Curie" for eight weeks in the spring
of 1938, but the movie didn't move into production and wasn't released until five years later with a completely different script. So that

summer Huxley was again looking for work. In the meantime, though, Heard had contacted the Vedanta Society and they were about to begin studying with its guru, Swami Prabhavananda.

There had been several movements in the nineteenth century of Western intellectuals and artists studying Vedanta. In Europe, Indian mysticism had been offered as the antidote to materialism and mechanization by such writers as Friedrich Schlegel, Novalis, and F. Max Muller, Oxford professor and editor of the famous *Sacred Books of the East* series. In the United States it had been embraced by the Transcendentalists, based on Ralph Waldo Emerson's study of Friedrich Schelling's *The System of Transcendental Idealism*, which relied on Vedantic concepts and which Emerson had learned of from Samuel Taylor Coleridge while visiting him in England in 1823. However, there was not a formal transplant of Vedanta from India to the United States until the very end of the nineteenth century. This was significant from a Hindu perspective as traditional Vedantists maintain that in order to study Vedanta mysticism properly one must have a guru. Only the guru, based on his elevated spiritual experience, can properly interpret the sacred texts. A guru is also trained in *sadhana*, the method required for direct spiritual insight. If the proper teacher is found then the spiritual path opens quickly for the student, which is why in India, as one contemporary scholar of Hinduism has put it, "The selection of a guru is more significant than the selection of a spouse."[2]


VEDANTA, AS A TRADITIONAL school of mysticism that advocates guidance by gurus, received a powerful boost in the United States in 1893 at the World Parliament of Religions in Chicago, when an actual Hindu guru showed up. Swami Vivekananda—tall, dark, handsome, and dressed in ochre robes and a white turban—drew rave reviews from the audience and, after the Parliament, traveled on a lecture tour that packed halls across the country. With Vivekananda we see the beginning of a formal guru tradition in America, a tradition whose efficacy other gurus, such as Paramahamsa Yogananda, would reinforce in the early twentieth century—and which later gurus, especially in the 1960s, would use to their advantage. The Vedanta Society of Southern California, where Huxley and Heard would study, was, in fact, a branch of the very organization Vivekananda had started in the United States.

Huxley and Heard (especially Huxley) were not sure that a guru was necessary, but felt that it would be interesting to explore the possibility. Both men agreed that to practice meditation correctly, it could certainly be useful to have guidance from someone who had been trained in the traditional techniques. Although the connection with the Vedanta Society was cause for optimism, Huxley was having trouble getting started due to his health. He had contracted bronchitis while on the peace tour and couldn't seem to shake it. He also was having problems again with his eyesight. The sunlight generally helped his eyes, but even with the strong California sun Huxley was definitely losing his sight. This, combined with the escalation of militarism in Europe, was pushing him into a depression.

After his lungs had cleared that fall, Huxley sought treatment for his eyes and began working with an experimental therapy called the Bates Method. The techniques used, developed by Dr. W.H. Bates, were, according to Aldous, "a perfectly rational and simple series of practices designed, first, to relax the eye and increase its circulation... second, to train the mind to interpret what the eye sends it and not to interfere with the functioning of the eye by straining or staring." Like the Alexander techniques he had experimented with to help his posture, the Bates Method involved strict physical retraining, and as often happened with Aldous when he was depressed, he focused on this new technique for self-improvement, using self-discipline not only to cure his eyes but also to prove to himself that progress of the individual is possible.

The therapy required several hours per day and six office visits per week but Huxley stuck to it, and he was encouraged by the results. His eyes did improve significantly and by the spring of 1939 Maria was calling the change a miracle. Aldous was reading without glasses or magnifiers, and his mood took an upswing. Maria wrote to a friend: "He has put on a lot of weight and with it a different air . . . I cannot explain. If you saw Aldous you would understand—he is somehow smoothed out. His moods and his depressions have smoothed out along with it . . . From having a vision of 15 percent he now has a vision of 50 percent and is making more rapid progress."

That same spring, in 1939, the Huxleys moved into a large house in Pacific Palisades, north of Los Angeles, where they would live for the next three years. Heard separated from them at that point and moved into a cottage on Chris Wood's property in Laguna Beach, but he and Aldous still saw each other regularly at the Vedanta center. Both had been ceremoniously initiated into meditation practice by Swami Prabhavananda, and were now, in Prabhavanada's eyes at least, his disciples. He had taught them the Vedanta Society's form of meditation, a visualization practice accompanied by the repetition of a Sanskrit mantra, a sacred name or syllable. The practice was said to quiet the mind and focus it, leading eventually to the experience of *samadhi* or oneness with Brahman.

In Vedanta it's believed that Brahman, because it is a oneness, cannot be experienced by the senses. Objects apprehended by the senses depend, implicitly, on duality—the observer sees the object, the observer hears the object, the observer feels the object, etc. For observation to take place there must be two things: the observer and the object (or, as in the case of intellectual knowledge, the thinker and the thought). But to experience that which transcends objects, the oneness itself, one cannot rely upon the senses. Brahman is known through an experience beyond duality, that is, by experientially awakening to the fact that it's being is identical with our own. It is not touched or heard, it is apprehended by *being* it, by being the oneness. When the mind becomes quiet, in fact, stopped, one sits inside one's true nature, synonymous with the true nature of the universe. One realizes that one's being is the being. Samadhi is the state the mystic Jan van Ruysbroeck once called "God contemplating God."

Heard and Huxley were making progress with their meditation practice and studying the texts of Vedanta with Prabhavananda. It was an exciting time for both men, but Huxley was becoming worried about Heard. Huxley had been somewhat distracted from his studies with Prabhavananda by his need to focus on his eye problems, and his natural skepticism caused him to keep a wary attitude toward his formal studies in Vedanta. Heard on the other hand seemed convinced that Prabhavananda had the secret he was looking for. He became increasingly focused on the guru's technique, spending long hours every day in meditation, rarely leaving his home. Huxley knew that Vedantists, along with other mystics, had sometimes been accused of quietism, of spending too much time in silent meditation while the problems of the world remained unsolved. Gerald, to Aldous's mind, was becoming too wrapped up in his private experience and Maria agreed. "He can't see us," she wrote to her sister, "because he will not leave his house for more than two hours at a time because of his meditations."

Aldous and Gerald never had a formal falling out or openly expressed animosity toward each other, but for a few years there was what Sybille Bedford has called a "lull" in their relationship. Heard's head-over-heels embrace at that time of the Vedanta Society and its practices was the central cause of the distance between them. His enthusiasm intensified that summer when Christopher Isherwood, another English novelist, also joined the Vedanta Society. Suddenly, Heard not only had his viewpoint encouraged, he had found another intellectual besides Huxley with whom to share his thoughts.

Already a famous writer, Isherwood, whom W. Somerset Maugham once described as holding "the future of the English novel in his hands," had first met Heard in London. He and the poet W.H. Auden, his lifelong friend and, at that time, lover, had visited the apartment of Heard and Chris Wood, Heard's lover. Isherwood, not yet interested in the metaphysical speculations that engrossed Heard and Auden, sat in another room and talked with Wood. However, over the years since that first visit, Isherwood had become deeply involved in the pacifist movement and, encouraged by a reading of Huxley's *Ends and Means*, wished to explore its spiritual foundations. He was eager to study meditation and Heard was eager for him to meet Prabhavananda. Later Huxley and Isherwood did become close friends (and even wrote a novel together) but at that first meeting, Huxley was a bit left out. "Oh yes, and I met Huxley," Isherwood wrote to a friend, "who is nice, but oh so bookish and inclined to be pontifical."[3]

110

Huxley would never formally sever his relationship with the Vedanta Society, and, in fact, contributed essays to some of their most important publications.[4] But he was having a hard time accepting Prabhavananda as his guru and with accepting gurus in general. Prabhavananda was quite open-minded, and usually dressed in a suit and tie but he was, in Isherwood's words, "strongly devotional," regularly performing ceremonies to his gurus and the Hindu gods. This did not fit well with Huxley's own spirituality. He did not condemn such practices openly, it was just that he didn't agree with them and felt uncomfortable kowtowing to gurus and gods. It seemed more Hindu, more of a cultural matter, than a necessary practice for self-realization. Heard interpreted Huxley's aloofness as part of his inability to commit to anything, but it was more than that. Huxley was committed to spiritual growth and it was his commitment to a particular ideal of spiritual growth that caused him to keep his distance.

He was uncomfortable intellectually with devotionalism. In *Eyeless in Gaza*, Anthony Beavis remarks, "Patanjali [who wrote the classic Hindu text of yoga philosophy] says you may believe in a personal God, or not, according to taste," but Huxley was certain that a personal god wasn't to his taste. He often argued that if worship is used as a means of spiritual growth it becomes difficult not to become trapped in the realm of division and duality. To raise the sacred up is simultaneously to put oneself down, to distinguish oneself as separate from the sacred oneness of Brahman. Huxley believed devotionalism was attractive because it allows the emotions to flow. By separating the oneness from oneself, usually by forming it into a god, it is possible to venerate and love it. However, he believed that for most people, veneration of the oneness in a personified form rarely leads beyond that form to the experience of oneness with it. More often it creates the illusion of an essential separation—that the god is something permanently and entirely "other" than the true self.

Huxley observed that personifying the Absolute as a god (whom he called the "Gaseous Vertebrate") often leads devotees of that god into conflict with those who personify the oneness differently, mistaking their particular personification of Brahman for the only proper or possible personification. Consequently, Huxley felt it best to focus one's will directly on trying to connect with the oneness itself. He believed this was more difficult than worship but far less confusing and problematic; people must accept that spiritual growth is difficult and put away their false idols. "Those who persist in having emotional relationships with God whom they believe to be personal are people who have never troubled to undertake the arduous training which alone makes possible the mystical union of soul with the integrated principle of all being."[5]

Later, in *The Perennial Philosophy*, Huxley would articulate the position he was working out in the early 1940s. He had already argued that when we turn a means into an ends we create a negative, unproductive transcendence of our self. When people make having a good time, working a job, acquiring wealth, or forwarding nationalism as ends in themselves, they transcend, on some level, their individuality. But, he argued, without working for a higher, more moral purpose, their efforts result only in vulgarity. This had been his position for many years, but beginning in the late1930s he expanded on this principle, speaking of it in spiritual terms. In *Ends and Means* he argued that "intelligence and charity" result from contact with the divine ground. Later, in *The Devils of Loudon*, published in 1952, he calls this an "upward self-transcendence," in contrast to the "downward self-transcendence" which he defines as "the escape beyond limits of the insulated ego, not to liberation but to enslavement." This, Huxley argues, occurs whenever we enshrine something less than the One, the Brahman. He came to believe that these negative transcendences are actually forms of idolatry which inevitably lead to vulgarity. In fact, all idolatry leads to vulgarity, and this is how he viewed the veneration of gods. It might make one feel better emotionally but it was enshrining a separation between oneself and the oneness. It was stopping at worship instead of integration. Again, it was confusing a means for an end.

In this same vein, Huxley argued that gurus could become false idols. This is an idolatry in which one lets go of the natural spiritual equality existing between all people (since everyone is essentially the One, after all) and sacralizes a particular person. Guruism then, if one isn't careful, simply becomes another means of false transcendence, giving over one's responsibility for personal growth to someone else. Furthermore, it gives the guru special privileges and powers and thus forms the foundation for religious hierarchies. Once a person has been singled out as more authoritative than others, an inner circle forms to protect the guru and to protect the interests of the inner circle. "Human beings are fallible, they make mistakes. Even with the best of intentions, things go wrong." To avoid constructing religious bureaucracies and hierarchies, Huxley thought it best to avoid setting up gurus. So he was perturbed by Prabhavananda's devotionalism and with Heard and Isherwood's devotion to him. Aldous could study Vedanta at the Vedanta Society but he could not embrace a traditional approach to enlightenment based on the guru/disciple relationship.

There were two other influences on Huxley at this time that cemented his disdain for gurus. The first was that Heard was becoming (and for a few years would remain) a guru himself. Gerald had always been charismatic and persuasive, and he was now gaining a reputation as a spiritual guide in his own right. In 1942 he created, with the flock gathering around him, a small institute in the hills behind Laguna Beach called Trabuco College as a monastic branch of the Vedanta Society. Huxley applauded the idea of a small group of people focusing diligently on their spiritual growth but he worried that things were instead focusing too much on Gerald himself. Huxley found this behavior pretentious on Heard's part and idolatrous on the part of his followers. Also significant at this time, and in this regard, was a friendship that Aldous had taken up with Jiddu Krishnamurti, another Indian holy man. Krishnamurti shared many of Huxley's ideas, including his dislike of devotionalism and gurus, and they mutually supported the concept of independent spiritual growth.

Krishnamurti wrote, after his first meeting with Huxley and Heard in 1938, "I liked them very much and it would be nice to continue further friendship with them."[6] The friendship with Huxley did continue, in fact, until Huxley's death, and had a formative effect on Aldous. Krishnamurti was to become the third friend in Aldous's life,

after Lawrence and Heard, to have a strong influence on his philosophical outlook. This, of course, is not to say that the influence only
went in one direction. All three men were certainly influenced by
Huxley as well. With regards to Krishnamurti specifically, Huxley
reinforced his dislike of formal religion and, on a personal note, got
him to learn the Bates Method of eye exercises, which Krishnamurti
then practiced all his life. By 1942 "Krishnaji," as Huxley called him,
had replaced Heard as Huxley's significant spiritual ally.

The story of Krishnamurti has to be one of the most unusual
biographies of the twentieth century, and it explains clearly why he
came to dislike gurus and organized religion. Born in India in 1895,
in a village in Tamil Nadu, as a young boy Krishnamurti moved with
his family to the oceanside, south of Madras, where one day, when he
was fourteen and walking on the beach with his brother, he unex-
pectedly met a man who would change his life. That man was C.W.
Leadbeater, an officer of the Theosophical Society, whose headquar-
ters stood nearby.

The Theosophical Society had originally begun in New York in
1875 as the brainchild of Madam Blavatsky, a Russian psychic, and
her wealthy associate, Colonel Olcott. The two leaders advocated a
belief in the miraculous and, from the society's founding, the congre-
gation was told that Blavatsky received spiritual messages by psychic
connection from a group of "ascended masters" living in the Himala-
yas of Tibet. In 1879, at the urging of these masters, Blavatsky,
Olcott, and others moved to India. When Blavatsky died, Annie Besant, an Englishwoman, became the prominent leader of the Society,
and it was to her that Leadbeater had brought the boy from the
beach. Leadbeater claimed that he psychically recognized the boy as
the next *jagad-guru*, the next "World Teacher," the savior whose coming is prophesied in a variety of world religions. Besant was convinced, and they made arrangements to adopt the boy and prepare
him to become the next Christ, or Burges.

Certainly there must have been something special about the boy.
Besant was astute and intelligent, and she herself found him compelling. She wasn't a charlatan (as most sources agree Blavatsky was),
and she had no intention of duping others. But she did believe that

the boy was an usual spiritual being, and she herself adopted him. Besant took over directing his education, eventually, in 1912, sending him to school in England. If he was going to reach a world audience, he would have to know something about the West, too. Krishnamurti remained in Europe for nine years, before returning to India in 1920 when he was twenty-six years old. Upon his return, Besant wished him to accept a leadership role in the Theosophical Society but he argued that he wasn't ready. One day, he was certain, he would be prepared as a vessel for his higher self (identified as Lord Maitreya, the Buddha-yet-to-come) to enter his body and lead the world to peace and light, but not yet.

Over the next few years Krishnamurti, usually living in either Holland or Ojai, California (where property and a cottage had been bought in his name), continued his training and preparation. Theosophists believe that it was during this period that he had his first clear moments of enlightenment. In 1922, after an experience which lasted three days, he wrote: "The fountains of Truth have been revealed to me and the darkness has been dispersed. Love in all its glory has intoxicated my heart; my heart can never be closed. I have drunk at the fountain of Joy and eternal Beauty. I am God-intoxicated."[7]

Despite these insights he was increasingly doubting his own divinity. By 1929, when he was thirty-four, Krishnamurti's doubts had become so acute that he formally resigned from being the next messiah and quit the Theosophical Society altogether. He soon was talking openly and vehemently against all organized forms of religion and spirituality. He was willing to continue as a teacher (wishing to "build a bridge for others to come over"), and kept a small organization to plan his engagements, but he maintained all his life that he was not a guru, often beginning his talks with the words: "We are going into this together. I am not your guru, you know . . ."

Of course, whether or not it's splitting hairs too finely to say that one is a teacher but not a guru is a point of contention—but Huxley felt comfortable with the distinction, defining it as a matter of choice. Krishnaji avoided adulation, asking his students to accept responsibility for their own spiritual growth, asking that they realize that when they accept someone as their teacher they do so by their own authority and choice. "I am just pointing out something to you," he once wrote, "you can take it or leave it, depending on you, not on me." In Krishnamurti, Huxley believed he had found an expert on the spiritual life, one who was enlightened and yet willing to meet him as an equal. "No one else reminds me so much of the Buddha," Huxley once remarked, but this Buddha, like the historical Buddha himself, wasn't asking for veneration. Aldous liked it that way.

The Huxleys moved in 1942 to a small ranch at Llano del Rio, in the Mojave Desert about fifty miles north of Los Angeles, where they could live frugally while waiting out the war. At Llano, Huxley, then forty-eight years old, lived a simple life and helped with the housework. He and Maria ate a plain vegetarian diet with no salt, and Huxley, when not writing, worked in the garden. Simple living became the foundation of their spiritual practice, and Maria wrote that they had "complete satisfaction with monotony." During this period, Aldous even learned, amazingly, to drive a car. His eyesight was far from perfect but he had achieved such results from the Bates Method that he felt confident enough to try. After practicing driving around their forty acres in the desert, he took his driving test and passed. Afterward, he felt compelled to give something back to Bates, and that same year he quickly wrote a small book, *The Art of Seeing,* outlining, endorsing, and defending Bates's techniques. The book was timely, as Bates had just come under attack. "Optometrists loathe the method," Aldous wrote to Julian, "because it endangers a hundred-and-fifty-million-dollar-a-year spectacle industry."

The Huxleys' remoteness at Llano somewhat restricted their social life but they would save their gasoline rations to drive out to Ojai to visit Krishnamurti whenever possible. Krishnamurti was often attended by Rosalind Rajagopal, the wife of his assistant, whom Maria usually visited with while the two men took long walks.

Having similar ideas about gurus and gods, the two men also shared similar views about the war raging in Europe and about war in general. But Krishnamurti had something new to add to Huxley's view of meditation. While still, at least at times, continuing to use the technique learned from Prabhavananda, Huxley felt no compulsion to limit himself to any particular meditation practice. In fact, he believed that people sometimes get too attached to their meditation techniques—again, making ends out of means, enshrining their practices as they do their gods and gurus. "To believe that their use either constitutes enlightenment, or guarantees it, is mere idolatry and superstition." Krishnamurti agreed with this, refraining from teaching any specific meditation practice. However, Krishnamurti did meditate and he recommended its practice. "Meditation is one of the greatest arts of life—perhaps the greatest, and one cannot possibly learn it from anybody. That is the beauty of it. It has no technique and therefore no authority."[8]

This, naturally, appealed to Aldous—but exactly what did it mean to meditate? Couldn't Krishna give any guidelines at all? "Look," Krishnamurti once explained to the writer Alan Watts, "on the one hand there must be the understanding that there is nothing, nothing, nothing, absolutely nothing that you can do to improve, transform, or better yourself. If you understand this completely you will realize that there is no such entity as 'you.' Then, if you have totally abandoned this ambition, you will be in the state of true meditation which comes over you spontaneously in wave after wave after wave of amazing light and bliss."[9]

What Krishnamurti was saying was that one doesn't have to contact the Brahman, it is already there; one must simply let go of the ego, which keeps the mind busy and distracted. In other words, when one free-falls without ego, leaving oneself open to being, that *is* meditation. As Huxley once put it: "If I cannot grasp *tatha* ["suchness," a Buddhist term for the ultimate truth] in activity, then obviously I must cease to be I, so that *tatha* may be able to grasp this ex-me and make it one with itself . . ." Krishnaji advocated that this practice required no special room or posture or incense. "You can do it at any time," Krishnamurti once explained at a lecture when someone asked about meditation.

> You can do it when you are sitting in a bus—that is, watch, observe. Be attentive to what is happening around you and what is happening in yourself. . . . You see, meditation is really a form of emptying the

117

mind of everything known. Without this, you cannot know the unknown. To see anything new, totally new, the mind must be empty of all the past. Truth, or God, or whatever name you like to give to it must be new, not something which is the result of propaganda, the result of conditioning. Truth is something living every day. Therefore, the mind must be emptied to look at truth.[10]

Trying to live consciously, being present by clearing the mind of cluttering thoughts, became Huxley's meditation of choice. During his visits with Krishnamurti, and their long walks, the two men often remained silent, each opening to the world around him. Huxley liked this practice—and liked that it was really not separate from life itself. One didn't have to stop doing anything to meditate, one simply had to try to be present in what one was doing. For Huxley, who was disposed toward improving the human situation, this was an antidote for both the overly busy mind and, simultaneously, for the quietism that some meditations might create. It was a way to be in the World but not be of it. Of the things Huxley inherited from Krishnamurti, his non-meditation, meditation practice seems most prominent.

ALDOUS AND MARIA had been sending money home to help their families, especially Maria's. They were also keeping Maria's niece, Sophie, then a young woman, until the war ended. Huxley's responsibilities had multiplied and he had to accept studio work to pay the bills. One outcome of this was that he received his first screen credits, helping to write film adaptations of Jane Austen's *Pride and Prejudice* starring Greer Garson and Lawrence Olivier in 1940, and Charlotte Bronte's *Jane Eyre* starring Orson Welles in 1944. Another outcome was that he had become friends with several members of the Hollywood crowd, including Charlie Chaplin, Paulette Goddard (Chaplin's wife at the time), Greta Garbo, Helen Hayes, and Orson Welles. (Huxley would sometimes joke with them about the fact that his brother, Julian, had already won an Academy Award for a short scientific film.)

In the summer of 1943 Huxley developed an allergy to a weed proliferating in the desert, and he and Maria would eventually have to sell the Llano property. Until then their remedy had been to take an apartment in Beverly Hills during the allergy season. This worked out nicely because they could more easily meet for lunch with friends such as Isherwood. Often friends from the Hollywood scene would join them. Huxley particularly liked Chaplin and Goddard—and, later, Goddard's second husband, Burgess Meredith—but certainly, as Ronald Clark, a biographer of the Huxley family, has explained, he was a strange match for Hollywood in general. Once, under a picture in *Variety* he was listed as "Al Huxley." When Sam Goldwyn first met him he is reputed to have said, "I'm delighted to meet you, Mr. Huxley, I understand you're practically a genius." One of the most interesting appraisals of Huxley ever came from Walt Disney, who once hired him to work on the script for *Alice in Wonderland.* "I hired Mr. Huxley to write a part for the character of Lewis Carroll [later cut from the script] and to supervise some of the touchier intellectual aspects of the story. But he was brainy. The second day he handed me a ten-page outline of what should be done. It was so literary I could understand only every third word. If you want to work in Hollywood it is not good to have brains."[11]

Huxley had several friends besides Krishnamurti, Isherwood and—when he saw him—Heard. Thomas Mann and several of the Germans who had been at Sanary were now, coincidentally, in Hollywood waiting out the war as well. Igor Stravinsky was also living there, and became very close to Aldous and Maria.

Huxley's publishing career took a slight turn for a short period; he wasn't doing much in the way of novels, saying that it was difficult to write fiction during a war. In 1939 he had put out *After Many a Summer Dies the Swan,* a parable about mortality and the vanities of wealth, based on the life of a Huxley acquaintance, William Randolph Hearst. The novel soon became a source for Orson Welles's own crack at Hearst in 1941 in *Citizen Kane.*

Aldous also had focused on and published a biography. Heard had suggested the idea of writing a study of Father Joseph, the eight-

eenth-century advisor to Cardinal Richelieu in the court of King Louis the Fourteenth. He and Huxley believed they had traced the origins
of the "present conflict" in Europe back to the Thirty Years War, a
war that Joseph had endorsed, and Huxley hoped to use the priest's
life as an object lesson. Father Joseph had been a mystic who later
became a political figure. Huxley used him to show that "Religious
people who think that they can go into politics and transform the
world always end by going into politics and being transformed by the
world." The book, *Grey Eminence*, was finished quickly, in only a few
months, and published in October 1941. Meanwhile, Huxley kept
working for the studios, "since books at the moment don't keep
wolves very far from doors."

While he was writing on and off for Twentieth Century Fox, in
February of 1944, Huxley finally finished a novel he had begun nearly
two years before, *Time Must Have a Stop*. The novel, later identified by
Huxley as his favorite, involves the story of a man, Eustace Barnack,
who devotes his life to pleasure and, as a wealthy man, can afford a
lot of it, but who, after his death, is traced through his sometimes
repentant but ultimately futile after-life experience (drawn closely
from Huxley's reading of *The Tibetan Book of the Dead*). Though Bruno
Rontini is the prophet of right vision in this book, the good man, it is
Barnack's nephew who delivers the moral: "The only hope for the
world of time lies in being constantly drenched by that which lies
beyond time." In Brahman, Huxley felt, time does have a stop, and
he continued to try to experience it.

*Time Must Have a Stop* was an important novel in Huxley's career.
Not only because it was one of his most popular, selling 40,000 copies in the United States in the first few weeks (and putting him, for
the first time, in a position of financial security), but because it is the
first novel in which his spiritual viewpoint shapes the entire narrative.

Unfortunately, some literary critics disliked the book for just that
reason. "What has happened to Huxley?" one of them asked. But
Huxley himself, then fifty years old, wasn't worrying about the critics.
He knew what he had wanted to say and he had said it. He accepted
his pronouncement—true or not—that he wasn't really a novelist
"but," as he wrote to a friend who admired the novel, "some other

kind of man of letters, possessing enough ingenuity to be able to simulate a novelist's behavior not too unconvincingly."[12] Huxley had also reached the conclusion that what primarily captured his attention was what was behind art, the source of "sweetness and light" more than its artifice. Novels were fine but he wanted to do more than writing novels would allow. Once, while visiting Heard at Trabuco College, in 1942, he had been asked to relate how he had become interested in mysticism, and his comment is revealing in this regard. Fortunately, Isherwood was in the audience and acted as secretary, taking the quote down verbatim:

> I came to this thing in a rather curious way, as a *reductio ad absurdum*. I have mainly lived in the world of intellectual life and art. But the world of knowing-about-things is unsatisfactory It's no good of knowing about the taste of strawberries out of a book. The more I think of art I realize that, though artists do establish some contact with spiritual reality, they establish it unconsciously. Beauty is imprisoned as it were, within the white spaces between the lines of a poem, between the notes of music, in the apertures between groups of sculpture. This function or talent is unconscious. They throw a net and catch something, though the net is trivial. . . But one wants to go further. One wants to have a conscious taste of these holes between the strings of the net.[13]

Huxley was moving away from novels as he had once moved away from poetry. He had only written three novels in the past ten years and, in fact, would only write three more before he died eighteen years later. Or, to put it another way, he wrote five novels in the first ten years of his career, and he wrote only six more during the next forty years. Huxley was interested in making another kind of mark on the world. He would continue his general vocation of being a self-appointed commentator on the state of culture and society, but he had yet to finish with his project of explicating a set of first principles that had been begun in *Ends and Means*. Now, in 1944, with the war still going on, he began writing the book (that would be published in 1945) that best defines his mature metaphysics, *The Perennial Philosophy*.

Huxley hadn't written a book of essays since *Ends and Means*, nearly seven years before. During this period he had compiled huge amounts of information about spiritual growth and the methods for attaining it. In fact, Huxley had suggested the project to himself as early as 1935. In *Eyeless in Gaza*, Anthony Beavis, while thinking about mysticism, writes in his diary, "There is a great work to be done here. Collecting and collating information from all these sources [Christian, Hindu, Buddhist, etc.]. Consulting books and, more important, people who have actually practiced what is in the books . . . In time, it might be possible to establish a complete and definitive *Ars Contemplativa*."

With *The Perennial Philosophy* Huxley finally got around to creating his anthology of mysticism, quoting from several religious traditions. His overall intent was to argue that there exists a particular mystical truth which is "the Highest Common Factor underlying all the great religions and metaphysical systems of the world." He arranged the book in such a way that he could group quotes from various spiritual traditions under particular subject headings, e.g., "God in the World," "Charity," "Truth," "Self-Knowledge," "Prayer," etc. The strong influence of Vedanta on him is evident; for instance, the first two headings are titled "That Art Thou," and "The Nature of the Ground." But in fact, though Huxley believed Vedanta was a clear revelation of truth (and his idea of a perennial philosophy resembles it more than any other tradition), he didn't believe that it was the only revelation of that truth. And this was important to him. Huxley didn't wish to claim exclusive allegiance to Vedanta. He believed that certain Buddhists also had a clear picture of the perennial philosophy—along with mystics of other traditions, such as Kabir, Rumi, and Lao Tzu.

*The Perennial Philosophy* also contains quotes from Western mystics: William Law (a favorite of Huxley's), Meister Eckhart, St. John of the Cross, St. Catherine of Genoa, St. Teresa of Avila, and others. Huxley wished to point out a deeper, pan-cultural, trans-cultural mystical tradition, not because Vedanta was wrong (in fact, Vedanta itself speaks of the Sanatana Dharma, the "Eternal Religion" which transcends all cultures) but because focusing on Vedanta alone might create the illusion that only by that path can enlightenment be reached. To mix metaphors, he was worried that those who were drinking from only one faucet might think they owned the town reservoir. Again, he was trying to clear away what he saw as a tendency toward idolatry—in this case, a kind of cultural myopia, which can lead to confusion and conflict. If the world was ever to live in peace it must learn to distinguish truth from how truth expresses itself in any particular culture at any particular time.

*The Perennial Philosophy*, still in print, is certainly one of Huxley's most interesting and important books. It is meticulously well-argued, well-presented, and compelling in content. Compelling, in fact, to the point where many have found themselves agreeing with Huxley, using his conclusions as a basis for finding meaning in their own lives. Huxley had been concerned about this—fearing that he might be opening himself up to charges of guruism. He knew that by trying to present the essence of mysticism he was setting himself up as someone who knew that essence. That's not how he wanted to present himself though. He had a theory about enlightenment but he didn't claim to be enlightened. He was simply using reason to argue a case. To safeguard against those who might think he was starting a new religion, a kind of "Huxleyism," he had his publisher include a disclaimer on the dust cover of the book.[14]

Huxley was simply presenting his best guess—arguing, as he had done in *Ends and Means*, that we are moving into darkness for lack of direct connection with the source of sweetness and light. His book wasn't intended as a bible. In fact, if people saw it that way they would be better off to throw it out. (Bibles, of any culture, he once wrote, are only "the strange, idolatrous over-estimations of words.") His hook, the disclaimer stated, was meant only as a guide. He didn't want readers to use it to find meaning in their life; he wanted them to use it to find their own meaning in life. Their own personal experience should be their ultimate guide to truth. Again, he was asserting his belief, reinforced by Krishnamurti, in freedom and personal choice.

Another instant hit, *The Perennial Philosophy* sold 23,000 copies in the first few weeks, encouraging Huxley that there was an audience for such a perspective. People who weren't looking for a guru, but who were looking, found the book an incredible inspiration. *Brave New World* had been Huxley's satirical description of the disease affecting humanity; *The Perennial Philosophy*—more than ten years in the making—was his view of an antidote. Today it is interesting to note that these two books, out of the fifty or so that he wrote, are the two that are continually in print, counteracting each other's presence as it were on the bookstore shelf.

# - 8 -

# SCIENCE, LIBERTY, AND PEACE

*What I'm Trying to persuade people is that they should think
in advance of what's going to happen. I mean the trouble is that one sees this
again and again that people have allowed themselves to be taken by surprise by
the advances in technology.*

—Aldous Huxley

IN THE SUMMER OF 1945 Aldous and Maria bought a small house 6,000 feet up in the Sierra Madre, in the village of Wrightwood. There they hoped to find solitude and relief from Aldous's allergies. Though it was beautiful and peaceful in the mountain forests, Maria also found it lonely and difficult. Matthew, now a U.S. citizen, was finishing college at Berkeley and the Huxleys were nearly two hours away from their other friends in Hollywood. After much urging, Maria convinced Krishnamurti to buy property near them and he and Rosalind visited from time to time from Ojai.

When summer had passed, both Huxleys realized how much they had taken on. Wrightwood was cold in the winter and their small house was dark and poorly built (the ceiling in Aldous's room was propped up with a tent pole). Aldous, for reasons that aren't clear, had stopped driving, and Maria had to do all the shopping and running around. In three short years, they would move again, this time back into Los Angeles, but for the present Aldous focused on writing and working with Krishnamurti's process of self-realization. Philosophically he was sticking to his "minimum working hypothesis," stated clearly in *Time Must Have a Stop*:

That there is a Godhead or Ground, which is the unmanifested principle of all manifestation. That the Ground is transcendent and immanent. That it is possible for human beings to love, know and, from virtually, to become actually identified with the Ground. That to achieve this unitive knowledge, to realize this supreme identity, is the final end and purpose of human existence.

He continued to write about his theories and experiments that year in several essays for *Vedanta for Modern Man*, edited by Isherwood and published by the Vedanta Society.

Many of his critics saw these essays as just more carrying on with the same old mumbo-jumbo he had been spouting for nearly ten years. As Isherwood later remarked, regarding prevalent perceptions of Huxley's mysticism, "His development was widely represented as the selling-out of a once-brilliant intellect."[1] In 1969, in a doctoral thesis for the University of London, David Bowering echoed this view, and gave the usual accusation, "One speculates whether mysticism, for Huxley, became a way of life or an escape from life."

Certainly Huxley himself did not feel that he was trying to escape from life. He wished to help humanity, to be of service, and he believed he was offering realistic, if uncommon, solutions. Even with regard to Vedanta itself, when one looks back over the whole body of his work, it does not seem that he was blindly "sold-out" to his metaphysical theories. His ideal of enlightenment was addressed as a "working hypothesis," not as a dogma to hide behind. The fact is that Huxley was too much his "grandfather's Enkel" (as Lawrence had put it), too much the empiricist, ever to allow himself to idolize his own theories. "If one is to explore the unknown," he once wrote, "one must not start by pretending that it is already known."

With regards to the world itself, it seems to have occupied Huxley excessively rather than not at all. If there was an ingrained tendency he had to fight, it was not mystical dreaminess but cynicism. Even in the years of his closest contact with Krishnamurti and the Vedanta Society, Huxley's sensitivity to the human condition constantly drove him toward pessimism. "What you say about the general hopelessness of the world at large," he wrote to Julian in 1945, "and the insolubility of its problems is painfully true." Huxley believed that his philosophical hypothesis offered a cure but he doubted strongly that anyone would accept it. He believed, as his letters make amply clear, that people would instead call it impractical and then set about the 'practical' business of killing each other. This often predisposed him to spells of gloom and (to use one of his own terns) "accidie," and though it is true that his metaphysics come out in his later novels, so does, and intensely so, his cynicism. In his novel *Time Must have a Stop*, published a year before *The Perennial Philosophy*, he writes about humans as robots, as creatures of pattern and stupidity:

> . . . human individuals, he was thinking. As living patterns in space, how incredibly subtle, rich and complex! But the trace they left in time, the pattern of their private lives—God, what a horror of routine! Like the repeats on a length of linoleum, like the succession of identical ornamental tiles along the wall of a public lavatory. Or if they did try to launch out into something original, the resulting scrolls and curlycues were generally atrocious. And anyhow most of them quickly ended in a smudge of frustration—and then it was linoleum and lavatory tiles, lavatory tiles and linoleum, to the bitter end.[2]

Even when Huxley was proposing solutions he was haunted, like his character Sabastian Barnack in the same novel:

> "Millions and millions," he whispered to himself; and the enormity of the evil seemed to grow with every repetition of the word. All over the world, millions of men and women lying in pain; millions dying, at this very moment; millions more grieving over them, their faces distorted . . . the tears running down their cheeks. And millions starving, millions

frightened, and sick, and anxious. Millions being cursed and kicked and beaten by other brutal millions. And everywhere the stink of garbage and drink and unwashed bodies, everywhere the blight of stupidity and ugliness. The horror was always there, even when one happened to be feeling well and happy—always there, just round the corner and behind almost every door.[3]

However, contrary to his critics' accusations, Huxley did not wish to escape the world, even when he found it ugly or when the "horror was always there." Huxley believed that only a coward would want to escape and only a Pollyanna *could* escape. Though he had his faults, he was neither of these. This is partially why Huxley, though a mystic, often reads more like an existentialist, such as Jean Paul Sartre or Carson McCullers. Ultimately, however, Huxley believed that even if the situation was hopeless—and he didn't always think so—one was morally obligated to try to improve it. From at least the time of *Ends and Means* in 1937 and the failure of the Peace Pledge Union that same year, Huxley held onto a specific kind of hope, which was not a species of pie-in-the-sky idealism. The viewpoint that tempered his cynicism and held it partially in check was like that best described by Vaclev Havel, who, while languishing in prison, once wrote:

Hope is an ability to work for something because it is good, not just because it stands a chance to succeed. It is not the same thing as optimism. It is not the conviction that something will turn out well, but the certainty that something makes sense regardless of how it turns out.[4]

Hope was why Huxley worked so diligently for solutions. Having this moral compass to guide him he could resist the extremes of melancholic existentialism and romantic dreaminess.

Extending an analysis of Huxley's metaphysics into his view of daily life, it is clear that though he didn't want to escape the world he did believe one should live free of it. In Vedanta he found what he hoped was a reconciliation, a way to be in the world but not of it. He strove for the enlightened non-attachment described in the *Bhagavad-Gita,* where Krishna advocates that Arjuna learn to know his true self, his Atman, so that he can then act in the world without attachment. Krishna does not ask Arjuna to detach himself from his dharma, his duty in life. Instead, he asks him to cultivate that aspect of his being, his consciousness, which both transcends and resolves the "realm of opposites," so that he can have the proper perspective on his actions. So that Arjuna can simultaneously be the ocean and the wave.

This was clearly Huxley's goal. He wasn't seeking to escape the world in the sense of running away from it. In fact, he believed that one must work in the world to attain true enlightenment. "Man must live in time in order to advance into eternity," he once wrote. Whether we agree with Vedanta or not, lack of understanding with regard to its metaphysics (and mysticism in general) has unfortunately led many critics to misread Huxley and his viewpoint. Milton Birnbaum says, "Huxley wants to be part of and apart from the human predicament," but he doesn't understand that Huxley found no contradiction in this dialectic.

IN *THE PERENNIAL PHILOSOPHY* Huxley articulated his set of metaphysical first principles. After that he worked out the specifics of his mature theory of art and esthetics—clearly expressed for instance in *Themes and Variations* published five years later in 1950. In the years immediately after the war, though, Huxley wrote mainly about pragmatic concerns of society, politics, and economic structures—hardly the concerns of an escapist. He never gave up believing that human problems must be attacked from every side and on every level, or that each aspect of the "multiple amphibian" must be addressed. Even in one of his 1945 essays for *Vedanta for Modern Man,* where he explains his metaphysics, he adds:

> This does not mean, of course, that an exclusive in-
> sistence on metaphysics will solve our problems. To

have a good philosophy is indispensable. But so are many other things. A good philosophy must be accompanied by good political institutions, good control of population, good agriculture, good soil conservation, good technology, good distribution of wealth, [and] good occupational therapy.

In his next book of essays, *Science, Liberty and Peace*, published a year after *The Perennial Philosophy*, and later in "The Double Crisis," from *Themes and Variations*, Huxley held forth on a variety of related issues, updating his thinking from the middle chapters of *Ends and Means*. He begins, and in a sense summarizes, *Science, Liberty and Peace* with a quote from Leo Tolstoy: "If the arrangement of society is bad (as ours is), and a small number of people have power over the majority and oppress it, every victory over Nature will inevitably serve only to increase that power and that oppression." Huxley felt that what was true in Tolstoy's time was still happening in his—in fact, more so, because of the increased power of technology. Applied science had mainly contributed to the "centralization of power in the hands of a small ruling majority," and he hoped to offer means by which "such tendencies may be resisted and ultimately, perhaps, reversed."

Huxley affirmed the maxim that the more absolute the power, the more absolute the corruption. To avoid totalitarianism and other consolidations of power, he advised that we practice more "Emersonian self-reliance," that we learn to live not only more self-sufficiently but more simply, using fewer natural resources and creating less waste. His ideal society is made up of many small, and largely autonomous, cooperative communities, practicing sustainable farming techniques. Ideally, these communities would not only have food security but also energy security, depending on small-scale applications of solar and wind technology. Aldous sounds very contemporary when he points out that solar and wind energy would not only supply "cheap and inexhaustible power," they would stop "the current jockeying for position in the Middle East" for "Arabian oil."

Industrial farming, he posited, has removed people from the land

and made them too dependent on centralized political and economic power. One result being that they have been forced into factory work and corporate jobs, which he considered ultimately impractical and inhumane. Impractical because this system largely only benefits the prosperous few, and inhumane because large-scale industrialization demands that the masses live with an unnatural pace and efficiency.

> Such a creature [as man] cannot, by its very nature, be continuously efficient. A machine, on the contrary, is designed to be efficient all the time. When a man is put in charge of a machine, or when he becomes part of some social or economic organization that is modeled upon the machine, he is compelled to be what it is not natural or normal for him to be. In more than moderate doses, efficiency is incompatible with humanity.[5]

Huxley argued in *Science, Liberty and Peace* that this dispensation has depended to a great extent on those in power promoting, in schools and the media, a dogmatic devotion to "progress," of which, platitudes aside, he saw few indications. A society can only be said to be progressing toward a goal if that goal is clearly articulated, but in the modern world Huxley did not believe that to be the case. Rather, Huxley believed society was seeing simply a repackaged religious longing for the promised land, believing out of historical momentum that "a glorious destiny awaits mankind," as it had once looked forward to heaven. "Faith in progress has affected contemporary political life by reviving and popularizing, in an up-to-date, pseudo-scientific and this-worldly form, the old Jewish and Christian apocalypticism."[6]

This religion of progress can continue, he argued, because the scientific community (to whom *Science, Liberty and Peace* was directly addressed) deludes the public into believing that their disciplines are objective and value-free, that technological progress is the natural direction of human evolution. Whereas, in reality, when science is applied to life it is never done so, nor can it be, in a way that is value-free.

The fact is, Huxley explained, scientists must choose what to investigate, and given that scientists must apply themselves in time, they must form priorities regarding what they most need to investigate, what best justifies the use of their time. Add to that, that every technology is created with some purpose in mind—to create some good, some advantage. These are all value judgments. Looking at the past two hundred years, Huxley saw that mainly the choices had been made which enhance nationalistic power and the centralization of wealth. Consequently, though scientists often argued that their actions were value-free, he saw them as forwarding religions of commerce and nationalism.

> The same men who reject as superstitious the belief in a transcendent and immanent spiritual Reality beyond and within phenomena, prove by their actions that they find no difficulty in worshipping as a supreme god whichever one of the world's fifty-odd nations they happen to belong to, and in accepting the infallibility of the local Foreign Office and the quasi-divinity of the local political boss.

For Huxley, the current economic and technological structures of the modern world were not only ideologically flawed; they were unsustainable because they did not consider the critical ecological issues of population growth, environmental degradation, and loss of natural resources. "Industrialism is the systematic exploitation of wasting assets. In all too many cases, the thing we call progress is merely an acceleration in the rate of that exploitation. Such prosperity as we have known up to the present is the consequence of rapidly spending the planet's irreplaceable capital."[7]

If we wish to live sustainably, Huxley argued, we must learn the complex systems of the natural world and find our place among them. He saw this as axiomatic. He saw it as not only practical but also, and implicitly, moral. "To any realistic observer it is surely obvious that not only do we have no right to treat living beings as things;

we have no right to treat even things as things. Things must be treated as though they were parts of a complex and beautifully coordinat-
ed living organism." On the other hand, "If, presumptuously imagining that we can 'conquer' Nature, we continue to live on our planet
like a swarm of destructive parasites—we condemn ourselves and
our children to misery and deepening squalor and the despair that
finds expression in the frenzies of collective violence."[8]

In Huxley's only novel from this period, *Ape and Essence,* published in 1948, he paints a dark picture of what an unregenerate
world could look like. He takes the reader to a future society living
on the Los Angeles plain after an atomic war, a society that in its bru-
tality far eclipses the one he had described in *Brave New World.* As
Sybille Bedford, explains, its community is "unspeakably bestial, unspeakably horrible. Affection, joy, compassion have withered, only
hunger, fear, lust, cruelty, malicious glee are left." At the start of the
story a narrator quotes Shakespeare, bracketing everything to come:

But man, proud man,
Drest in a little brief authority,
Most ignorant of what he is most assur'd.
His glassy essence—like an angry ape,
Plays such fantastic tricks before high heaven
As make the angels weep.

Here Huxley is again presenting a cautionary tale—and one example of what in his dark moments he feared is an inescapable human pattern. But in *Science, Liberty and Peace* and in "The Double Crisis," he was offering solutions and this is significant to remember. He
did not argue against technology; he called for appropriate technology. He pointed out that applied science had been applied mainly to
equipping large concerns with the expensive machinery of mass production and mass distribution, "whereas it could as easily equip the
individual, the family or the small cooperative community" with
"cheap and simple, but effective, means of production for their own
subsistence." And then he suggested how.

Jiddu Krishnamurti, 1935

(Photo by Ralph Gardner
Krishnamurti foundation of America)

Swami Prabhavananda
and Aldous Huxley
circa 1960

Swami Prabhavananda, Aldous Huxley,
and Christopher Isherwood

(Vedanta Society of Southern California)

Gerald Heard and Chris Wood in front of the
Vedanta Society's temple in Hollywood, 1948

(Vedanta Society of Southern California)

T.S. Eliot, who became close
friends with Aldous Huxley.

(National Archives)

Aldous Huxley (second from right) and Christopher Isherwood (far right) entering the Vedanta Society's temple in Hollywood.

(Vedanta Society of Southern California)

Josephine MacLeod, Aldous Huxley (in trademark white socks), Carrie Mead Wyckoff (a Vedanta nun known also as Sister Lalita), Maria Huxley, and Swami Prabhavananda at the Hollywood center of the Vedanta Society, 1947.

(Vedanta Society of Southern California)

Aldous Huxley and Maria Huxley (facing front)being greeted at the Vedanta Society by Josephine MacLeod and Swami Prabhavananda 1947.

(Vedanta Society
of Southern California)

When he finished describing his ideal community, he also outlined ways in which change might be affected within the current system. For example, we could better ensure that science and technology are used for sustainability, liberty, and peace if governments created formal committees to assess when, if ever, new technologies are allowed to emerge. These committees, when reaching their decisions, should consider all impacts on the quality of life—not just those that quickly and superficially bolster the Gross National Product. In addition to this safeguard, he recommended that all scientists begin their careers as do doctors, by taking a sort of Hypocratic oath, swearing not to use their knowledge in ways that are destructive to life or that enslave people.

Huxley was arguing that we simply could not go on as we presently were. "The human race is passing through a time of crisis, and that crisis exists, so to speak, on two levels—an upper level of political and economic crisis, and a lower level of demographic and ecological crisis." The lower-level crisis should not be ignored because it is "bound to exacerbate the crisis on the political and economic levels." In other words, as human populations grow and resources wane, millions of people will be desperate for food. Power must always be tempered by the need for sustainability. For Huxley this was simply being practical. As Aldous had argued that nationalism is a false god, so he argued that science is. Science and technology are means that can—but won't necessarily—be used to help humanity. Glorifying them as implicitly good is idolatry, making them ends in themselves. The true goal must begin with people and their needs.

One criticism of Huxley's analysis that bears consideration has been that his recommendations, though interesting, were only superficially developed. This is certainly true, and it is endemic to his analyses of many topics outside of mysticism. In many ways he was simply too profoundly curious about everything to focus on any particular set of issues or topics. June Deery, a recent commentator on Huxley's views, has characterized his investigations, saying: "Instead of digging deep in a small plot, he travelled extensively over a wide surface."[9] But this was Huxley's conscious process. He was not an expert in any particular scientific discipline and believed he was of best service as a generalist. Too little attention, he said, was being given in academic institutions to interdisciplinary knowledge and too little attention was being given to alternative thought in general, so that he, as a generalist and as a man of belle lettres, had something unique to offer in the search for meaning. Someone, he reasoned, should be looking into the blind spots. In truth, it is for his work in those areas that Huxley—as something other than a novelist—is largely remembered today.

Some critics have argued that Huxley was fickle in the way that he moved around from topic to topic. Charles M. Holmes has said that when Huxley resumed talking about art in *Themes and Variations* he dropped mysticism for the time and was "looking around and not above." This is true in a sense (in that he was writing about a different subject) but given the nature of Huxley's spirituality, and his loyalty to it, it isn't the best assessment. It's true that when discussing art—or society or war or the population issue—Aldous was "looking around," but his general tendency was then to set the look "around" within the look "above." Yes, he discussed art in *Themes and Variations*, but he did so relative to his spiritual theories. In *Science, Liberty and Peace* he discussed how to create a sustainable society but then explained how that would facilitate the realization of our "final end" as citizens and individuals.

> Sorrow exists within all fields and can be ended within all fields. Nevertheless it remains true that some fields put more obstacles in the way of individual development and individual enlightenment than do others. Our business, as politicians and economists, is to create and maintain the social field which offers the fewest possible impediments to the ending of sorrow.[10]

What was consistent in Huxley as he moved around in his analysis was the desire to improve the human condition and to see spiritual awakening as fundamental to that. Wherever he looked, he looked only to help, and whatever he found he tended to place in relationship to his first principles. As a generalist Huxley hoped to add this overarching level of moral concern even as he discussed problems at every level. No culture exists without moral and esthetic values; Huxley simply chose to ground his in his perennial philosophy.

IN THE LATE FORTIES Huxley's health was stable and his personal life generally pleasant. He and Maria had finally come down from their mountain and in for a landing and had moved into a pleasant house on North Kings Road in Los Angeles. Matthew had finished his degree at Berkeley and now, engaged to be married, had gone off to New York for a job.

It was during this period that Huxley wrote the only screenplay for which he received exclusive credit. *A Woman's Vengeance* (starring, in 1948, Charles Boyer and Jessica Tandy) was based on his short story "The Gioconda Smile." Huxley was pleased with the result (though not with the title) and had great respect for its director, Zoltan Korda. In a letter to Anita Loos, he praised Korda but found himself complaining about people in the movie industry who believed that money conveys expertise. "He [Korda) is a nice, intelligent fellow and we were able to co-ordinate our respective specialties of writer and director without the interference of a producer. Consequently, the work was done quickly and efficiently, without being held up by retired button-manufacturers using the Divine Right of Money to obstruct the activities of those who do the actual work."[11]

Aldous's relationship with Krishnamurti continued. In fact, in several ways it deepened. Huxley was, according to Mary Lutyens, Krishnamurti's biographer, the one who actually started Krishnamurti in his writing career. His prior publications had been transcripts of lectures he had given, but Aldous thought he might make his points more clearly in a book. When *The First and Last Freedom* was published in 1954, it featured a forward by Aldous Huxley. Their relationship had also become more cemented after Aldous and Krishnamurti had begun a school together in Ojai in 1946.

Both men were staunch advocates of primary education, and they hoped to create a primary school that considered the whole human being, not just the intellect. Their goal was for a curriculum that would teach students values beyond the status quo—as Huxley was always lamenting that the current educational system was "the state's most effective instrument of universal regimentation." The school was called Happy Valley School and its motto was *Aun Aprendo*, "I am still Learning." At the first commencement, in 1951, Aldous gave the key address, urging the children to remember the school's motto, and pointing out, "In all too many cases men and women do not wish to go on learning." To make his point, that people too often become set in their ways, he recited the old limerick about the man who said, "Damn, It is borne in on me that I am,/ a creature that moves in predestined grooves./I'm not even a bus, I'm a tram!"

Along with their close relationship with Krishnamurti, Maria and Aldous also developed further their friendships with Stravinsky and Isherwood, who had formed their own friendship and who, biographies being accurate, sometimes enjoyed going to the beach together and getting drunk. Isherwood, now a U.S. citizen, had, as a pacifist, performed alternative service during the war with a Quaker relief organization. On his return to Hollywood in 1944, he and Aldous had cemented their appreciation and affection for each other. Isherwood was still devoted to Prabhavananda and editing books for the Vedanta Society (with which Aldous also helped), and Huxley, now more emotionally tied to Isherwood, found himself more tolerant of his friend's devotionalism. Huxley had long considered Isherwood the better novelist; he was also now finding more respect for him as a person.

Stravinsky was very dear to Maria especially, who found him "elfish" and sweet. She wrote in 1951, describing the maestro's appearance one evening, "Stravinsky arrived in an enchanting costume. . . in little blue jeans, and a blue jean zipper jacket open on a deep red wine jersey and silk scarf tied with a pin. He looked enchanting and was really pleased with himself. I must not forget the always white socks and sandals."[12] Aldous found Stravinsky more fascinating than charming, admiring, and perhaps coveting, his musical genius, "What does it actually feel like to think in terms of melodies and harmonic progressions?" he wondered. Stravinsky was also fascinated with

Huxley—not because Aldous was knowledgeable about music, which he was, but because he was knowledgeable about everything. In fact, Stravinsky once described Aldous as "a kind of handy neighborhood university." When Stravinsky had a question, he would call Aldous and play stump the professor—for instance, once ringing him up to ask about the origin and history of scissors.

Another friend from this period was Edwin Hubble, the astronomer for whom the space telescope is named. Aldous and Maria were close to both Hubble and his wife, Grace. Edwin Hubble, at six-foot-five inches tall, was a giant like Huxley. He had played soccer at Oxford with Aldous's brothers (while on a Rhodes scholarship) and was an inveterate Anglophile. Huxley, with his King's English and perfect manners—not to mention a fascination for science—was an ideal companion for the astronomer. Hubble worked at the nearby Mt. Wilson Observatory, and when the Huxleys first met him, he was already famous for proving that there are many galaxies beyond our own, greatly enlarging our conception of the size of our universe. He had also established that the universe is expanding, and he was quite fond of discussing such matters with Aldous—sometimes to the consternation and boredom of Stravinsky, Isherwood, and others.

In the late 1940s *Vogue, Life,* and *Time* all published stories on Huxley and, as David Dunaway points out in *Huxley in Hollywood,* when the *Life* article came out, "for a brief week, every barbershop and dentist's waiting room from sea to shining sea sported Aldous's picture."[13]

Huxley's life remained generally good, but work in Hollywood was slowing down, at least for Aldous. Consequently, he was toying with the idea of reworking the screenplay for his short story, "The Gioconda Smile" ("Gioconda" is the title of the young woman in Da Vinci's *Mona Lisa*), making it into a play for the stage.

This was one of the projects Huxley was working on when on January 30, 1948, he learned that Mohandas Gandhi, one of his greatest heroes, had been assassinated by a religious fanatic. Huxley, in his early years, had not always had nice things to say about the Mahatma, but as Huxley embraced pacifism, and then later Vedanta, he became impressed with Gandhi's resolve to oust the British through nonviolent means—proving to the world that pacifist methods could be effective. The assassination left Huxley bitter, and he vented his feelings by quickly adding comments about the incident to his novel *Ape and Essence*, which was largely finished at the time. He has the novel begin on the day Gandhi died, and in the first dialogue of the book a character comments sarcastically on the murder, "Gandhi was a reactionary who believed only in people. Squalid little individuals governing themselves, village by village, and worshipping the Brahman who is also the Atman. It was intolerable. No wonder we bumped him off." His cynical feelings at this time were further reinforced by the irony of Gandhi's funeral. In "A Note on Gandhi" for the Vedanta Society's magazine he pointed out that the Mahatma's body had been carried to his cremation on a weapons carrier, and that there were tanks and soldiers in the procession. "All these instruments of violent coercion were paraded in honour of the apostle of non-violence and soul-force. It was an inevitable irony." Huxley's use here of the word "inevitable" is particularly telling of his basal viewpoint.


WITH THE BEGINNING OF THE 1950s Huxley was generally accepted as a revered commentator on modern life, and soon he would be broadcasting his viewpoints in a regular feature for *Esquire*. In 1950 he traveled to England (for only the second time in thirteen years); while there he visited many friends, including "Tom" Eliot and Raymond Mortimer. Clearly, any animosities that were once felt toward him for living elsewhere during the war or maintaining a strict pacifism were now forgotten. (As Ronald Clark once put it, there had been some who, when the war became inevitable, disliked Huxley for "sticking to his lack of guns.") Also during this trip he and Maria had a happy reunion with Aldous's brother, Julian, and his wife, Juliette. Aldous and Julian had remained close all these years (unlike his relationship with his sister Margaret, a school teacher, with whom he does not seem to have had much of a relationship) and would continue to be all of their lives and were, in many ways a team. Reading their long letters it can be seen not only how much they respected each other's viewpoints but how much their viewpoints had in common.

Julian was an enormous source of scientific information for Aldous (it was Julian who first read Carr-Saunder's pioneering work *The Population Problem* when it came out in 1922, which strongly influenced him—and through him Aldous). Julian was also, in 1950, the recently appointed president of the British Humanist Association and he looked to his younger brother as a moral and spiritual sounding board on many issues. They didn't always agree but they always shared their ideas and managed to find common ground. Important in this regard is the fact that Julian also had recently become very influential—and not just in the British Humanist Association.

After the war, in the spring of 1946, the United Nations had begun plans for educational and cultural reconstruction. Julian became the first director-general of that plan, called UNESCO, the United Nations Educational, Scientific, and Cultural Organization. Julian saw this as a chance to forward his own secular humanism and Aldous encouraged him and made recommendations. "I wonder," Aldous wrote, in his letter of congratulations on the directorship,

> if there is any hope, through UNESCO, of persuading the technologists, when they apply the results of pure science to industry, to remember that the Sabbath was made for man and not vice versa; that human beings with certain physical and psychological needs come first and that applied science should serve those needs and those human beings and should not compel the human beings to be the slaves of applied science and its capitalistic or governmental owners and managers.

The fifties would be a decade of triumph for Huxley, a decade in which his experiments with spirituality and LSD would bear significant fruit. But the decade didn't begin well and it was punctuated by tragedies small and large. Stopping in New York on his way back from London in the fall of 1950 he found out that things were not going as planned with the production of the screenplay for "The Gioconda Smile." In fact, the actors were "at daggers drawn with the director-producer," and the play quickly flopped. Soon after his return to California Huxley became seriously ill. What started out as a flu had by winter settled into further problems with his bad eye, which became swollen and painful. Soon the iritis was so acute, as it had been when he first lost his sight, that there was even talk of removing the eye. (There was concern that it would infect his good eye and he might become completely blind.) He suffered along, physically and emotionally, for nearly six months—which was quite hard on Maria, too, as Aldous sometimes became irritable and difficult. "He was really so rattled," Maria later wrote to their son Matthew, who was now married and living in New York. "It really was horrible." Fortunately, the eye eventually cleared and by late summer, 1951, there was no danger of losing it. With the return of health Huxley's spirits improved.

Huxley's spirits got even more of a boost that October, with the birth of his grandson, Mark Trevenen Huxley. Both first names had been suggested by Aldous—"Mark," inspired by the fact that he had named his own son after an apostle, so why not continue the trend? The second name, Trevenen, was the one Aldous most preferred, on the merit of its being "euphonious" and "commemorating a very rare being, whom we all loved." Aldous was a happy grandfather and, for a time, he took to calling Maria "Granny."

Now that his eye was better he was writing again, continuing work on a biographical/historical treatment of the circumstances surrounding a series of supposed demonic possessions involving nuns and their confessor in France during the seventeenth century. The book, published in 1952 as *The Devils of Loudon*, became a forum in which Huxley shared his latest ideas (for instance, about hypnotism), along with the direct circumstances of the nun's possessions and the Inquisition's investigations of them. As Dunaway has pointed out in *Huxley in Hollywood*, the book was meant to shed light on the dangers and absurdities of the witch hunting for "Commies" then going on in Hollywood—which directly affected Huxley (who, though not an avowed Communist, was considered a "fellow traveler" with the "commies"), along with several of his friends, including Chaplin.[14]

In the first month of 1952 the family's concern shifted from Aldous to Maria, who was in the hospital to have a cyst removed from behind her right breast. "The limelights have been on me," she wrote to Matthew, "and you know I make faces." The biopsy proved the cyst to be malignant but Maria bore it stoically and decided against telling Aldous about the seriousness of her condition. Thinking it would be too much of a shock after what he had recently been through with his eye, she also thought perhaps there was a chance of a cure. She continued in her letter to Matthew, "I shall recover 100%, there will be no recurrence." Unfortunately, there was.

# - 9 -

# THE DOORS OF PERCEPTION

The real voyage of discovery consists not in seeking
new landscapes but in having new eyes.
—Marcel Proust

AI,DOUS WROTE TO MARIA'S SISTER, Jeanne, on January 26, 1952, that "Maria is home and is getting on remarkably well." But her strength was in fact slow to return. If this worried Maria she didn't show her concern to Aldous, and as soon as she could resume a normal life she did. They often got together on Tuesday evenings with friends. These meetings were largely social events—sometimes hosted by the Huxleys but often involving going out to attend lectures or visit psychics. "Among our diversions in those days," Anita Loos later said, "were any number of experiences among the mystics of that world center of mumbo jumbo."[1] For Loos, Paulette Goddard, Burgess Meredith, Greta Garbo, or others who took part in these get-togethers, they were largely entertainments. The Huxleys also tended not to take them seriously, but .Aldous was chronically on the lookout for things that could be of use. He didn't dismiss everything unusual as either quackery or charlatanism. In fact, since so many others did, he had decided to be a self-appointed researcher of those places where no one else bothered to look. he once wrote, defending his position:

> All sorts of cultists and queer fish teach all kinds of
> techniques for achieving health, contentment, peace

148

of mind; and for many of their hearers many of these techniques are demonstrably effective. But do we see respectable psychologists, philosophers and clergymen boldly descending into those odd and sometimes malodorous wells, at the bottom of which poor Truth is so often condemned to sit? Yet once more the answer is, No.[2]

Huxley thought that there were many precedents for being open-minded in this regard; for example, in 1848, a British physician, Dr. James Esdaile, had published *Mesmerism in India* about his use of hypnosis as anesthesia. Esdaile had performed more than three hundred operations without anesthesia and claimed an extraordinarily low death rate from post-operative shock (the average in Britain then was twenty-three percent of all cases, while Esdaile's rate, which could easily be verified, was only five percent). Aldous found it unconscionable that Esdaile's work had been derided and dismissed on what he believed to be, largely irrational, unscientific grounds. He wondered how many other Esdailes there were, labeled as kooks and left at that.

In *Themes and Variations* Huxley wrote about the history and theory of hypnotism itself, believing that its scientific details should be made known. Huxley saw promise in hypnotism for a variety of uses including psychological research as well as medical treatment. But his interest in exploring the unusual was not limited to hypnotism—all manner of alternative therapies and parapsychological phenomena caught his attention. Tuesday meetings included looking into Scientology, animal magnetism, ESP, telekinesis, psychic prediction, seances, and other "mumbo jumbo."

Some scholars and critics have tried to dismiss Huxley's interest in these fields, suggesting that it came out later in his life either as a desperate reaction to his wife's failing health or as a by-product of his mystical woolly-mindedness. But Huxley had published his first article on hypnotism back in 1937. He never became enamored though of any particular therapy or practice, often joking in letters about the absurdity of one or other of them. As Maria explained in a letter describing some of the therapies they were then trying, "Do not think that we are Faddists. Less than ever."[3]

Huxley was, and would always remain, a rationalist—once commenting in *Themes and Variations*, "When reason sleeps, the absurd and loathsome creatures of superstition wake and are active, goading their victims to an ignoble frenzy." The "divine ground," as he conceived it, transcends the world apprehensible with science, and the ultimate truth inspired by contact with that ground is experiential rather than reason-based, but neither of those phenomena contradict science and reason—and, for Huxley, they must not. Consequently, he believed that telepathy and clairvoyance were possible, though he did not believe in the supernatural. His view was that there are things in the world, natural (not supernatural) things, which might be misunderstood or overlooked, and these he wished to bring to light.

In his informal investigation of the paranormal, he was still very clear that what one really needed to strive for spiritually was enlightenment and not the lesser spiritual powers of the mind. These might have some utility or provide evidence for a new understanding of the mind or the universe, but they couldn't bring the ultimate insight and serenity promised by Huxley's "timeless moment of conscious experience." "He maintained a classic spiritual hierarchy, with contemplatives occupying the upper ranks and the "infinitely less valuable intuitions of psychics assigned to the lower depths."[4] But still the lower depths deserved to be studied; something useful might be found, and anything that could help, even if only in a small way, should be brought to light. Huxley was consequently very supportive of his friend Dr. J.B. Rhine, the ESP researcher at Duke University, and encouraged him to publish an anthology of serious work on parapsychology for the popular press. In January of 1954, Huxley published his own report in *Life* magazine, "A Case for ESP, PK, and PSI," in which he praised Dr. Rhine.

Entertainment was the main reward of the Tuesday night sessions, true; but Huxley believed he did find a few valuable insights, particularly among the therapies that claimed to move one toward spiritual awakening. Huxley, like Krishnamurti, saw no reason to enshrine traditional yogas and meditations, believing it was certainly possible that someone might stumble onto other methods perhaps even more scientific and efficacious. He and Maria tried many systems, including dianetics, the practice of working with an "auditor" to supposedly remove psychological blocks to self-realization. This system had been developed by L. Ron Hubbard, the founder of the Church of Scientology, whom Huxley found "a very queer fellow—clever, rather immature . . . and in some ways rather pathetic," but who Huxley also believed made several valid points regarding psychological limitations. The Huxleys also tried Entelechy Therapy, a technique developed by A.L. Kitselman, who had studied Indian religions, especially Theravada Buddhism, and combined their metaphysics with auto-hypnosis. "E therapy" involved using hypnosis to request help from one's own subconscious and inner self. Aldous explained it as "a collaboration between the person, who is trying to get out of the way as a self and establish contact with the beneficent non-self, and an observer who asks questions and otherwise provides help."

Huxley never found himself convinced of any one technique and, in fact, often experimented by combining elements from each of them. For a time he tried combining aspects of dianetics with E therapy, specifically, with autosuggestion, to create a personal practice he thought delivered "a high degree of relaxation, mental and physical." He also tried using posthypnotic suggestion to quickly get back to the state of ego release and peace he felt he had achieved in his freeform, Krishnamurti-inspired meditations.

How effective any of these techniques were is, of course, difficult to say; however, their effectiveness seems to have been demonstrated, to some degree, in Huxley's own personality. Increasingly, according to those closest to him, Aldous was becoming like one of the wise men (e.g., Rampion, Dr. Miller, or Bruno Rontini) from his novels. As early as 1948, Cyril Connolly had remarked, in the London *Picture Post*, "If one looks at his face one gets first an impression of immense intelligence, but this is not unusual among artists. What is much more remarkable and almost peculiar to him is the radiance of serenity and loving-kindness on his features; one no longer feels 'what a clever man' but 'what a good man,' a man at peace with himself."

In the nineteen-fifties this effect seems to have grown stronger. Maria, writing to her sister Jeanne in 1952, said that Aldous was "transformed, transfigured," and that "this change has been working for a very, very long time but the result has suddenly exploded—and I say exploded." And Bedford, describing Huxley in 1954, while he was visiting her in Rome, remarks: "He was as gentle as he had been in all his phases, yet behind it one felt authority. And there was a sleekness, a smoothed-outness; he was glowing with it, as it were, and this had an extraordinary peace-inducing effect."[5] This last comment came the summer after Aldous had tried psychedelic drugs. Huxley often was, and still is, rather carelessly connected with drug research and psychedelic mysticism, without understanding his motives and conclusions.

IN 1952 ALDOUS HAD READ an article on psychological medicines in the *Hibbert Journal* by two authors, one of whom was Dr. Humphry Osmond, a young British doctor working in Canada. Osmond had been doing research on mescaline, a synthesized form of the psychoactive substance found in the peyote cactus, and his results fascinated Aldous. Huxley wrote to Osmond, and Osmond, by coincidence a fan of Huxley's, responded. Fortuitously, Osmond was soon due to attend a symposium in Los Angeles sponsored by the American Psychiatric Association and so perhaps, Osmond wrote, he and Huxley might get together then. Huxley was delighted and invited Osmond to stay with him and Maria during the symposium. Osmond agreed.

During that visit Osmond and Aldous began a friendship and close correspondence that would last the rest of Aldous's life. Huxley appreciated Osmond's open-mindedness and Osmond was impressed with Huxley's pragmatism. "In spite of remarks that I sometimes heard about 'unfortunate mystical trends in his later years' I found him, both then and subsequently, shrewd, matter-of-fact and to the point."[6] Early in the visit, Osmond brought Aldous with him to the symposium. Many Freudians were in attendance and, Osmond later related, that whenever Freud's name was mentioned, Aldous—always looking to debunk false idols—began "crossing himself devoutly."

After the meeting and back at the house, Huxley and Osmond discussed mescaline research, particularly as it impacted spiritual experience. Huxley was already familiar with the history of this research, which dated back to the 1880s. Louis Lewin, a German toxicologist, had first experimented with peyote (synthetic mescaline had not yet been produced), and concluded that it possessed "a high degree of scientific interest for general research." He believed that the ethnologist might find in it the key for understanding the origins of religious experience. Lewin had spurred interest among other scientists and intellectuals—including K. Beringer, S. Weir Mitchell, and Havelock Ellis, who shared peyote with the poet William Butler Yeats. Huxley had read Ellis's comments at least as early as 1943, and they encouraged him. Ellis wrote that peyote did not impair the functioning of his intellect and is "of all this class of drugs the most purely intellectual in its appeal. . . . On this ground it is not probable that its use will easily develop into a habit."[7]

William James was another researcher of peyote with whom Aldous was familiar. James, the father of American psychology and the brother of the novelist, Henry James, founded the psychology department at Harvard University and is best known today for his landmark book, *The Varieties of Religious Experience.* James experimented with peyote and nitrous oxide and believed that important levels of intelligence (hidden from the narrow, gauged, everyday mind) could be awakened by use of drugs. "Our normal waking consciousness, rational consciousness as we call it, is but one special type of consciousness, whilst all about it, parted from it by the filmiest of screens, there lie potential forms of consciousness entirely different."[8] Reflecting on his drug experiences, he once wrote, "They all converge towards a kind of insight to which I cannot help ascribing some metaphysical significance."

Huxley was interested in trying mescaline himself and found no reason to dismiss chemically induced mysticism as necessarily fallacious as some people did. "The breathing disciplines of yoga, after all," he wrote, "altered the concentrations of carbon dioxide in the blood and these changes were simultaneous with the new vision of reality to which the yogi attained; the abstinence of those who fasted produced chemical changes which were apparently concurrent with voices heard and visions seen. What, after all, was so unlikely in the suggestion that chemical compounds might open the door to comparable experience?"[9]

Osmond had brought some of the drug, not yet illegal, to Los Angeles so Huxley could try it. Osmond had been working mostly with mentally disturbed patients, but because of consistent reports of spiritual experience he wanted to accumulate information from someone who had a complex understanding of mysticism. Would someone like Huxley reify William James's findings? Would he think the experience metaphysically significant? "In spite of seventy years of mescalin [generally spelled without an e at the end at the time] research," Huxley wrote of Osmond's work, "the psychological material at his disposal was still absurdly inadequate, and he was anxious to add to it. I was on the spot and willing, indeed eager, to be a guinea pig. Thus it came about that, one bright May morning [1953], I swallowed four-tenths of a gram of mescalin dissolved in half a glass of water and sat down to wait for the results."[10]

Osmond gave Huxley the drug with a bit of apprehension. Huxley was nearly fifty-nine years old but this wasn't the problem. Mescaline is not very toxic and Aldous was in reasonably good physical condition. The worry was about the psychological effect. "Aldous and Maria would be sad if it did not work," Osmond later said, "but what if it worked too well?" However, he soon learned his fears were groundless. And thus began one of the most interesting and controversial experiments in the history of Western psychology—one that has historical significance in its marked impact on the youth culture of the 1960s and the scientific research into psychedelics that has subsequently taken place.

The results of that first experiment were published, in 1954, in Huxley's *The Doors of Perception*, a small book of seventy pages that has had a very large effect in the history of drug research. Huxley borrowed his title from William Blake's poem, *The Marriage of Heaven and Hell*, in which Blake writes, "If the doors of perception were cleansed everything would appear to man as it is, infinite."

Physiologically speaking, what happened to Aldous that day, or what happens to anyone under the influence of psychedelics, is still not completely clear. Philosophically speaking, there is even more uncertainty. Aldous, with Osmond's help, formulated his own functional theory, which he presented in his book. There he explains that he agrees with "the eminent Cambridge philosopher" Dr. C.D. Broad who believed that Henri Bergson, the French philosopher, was probably right and that, in Broad's words:

> the function of the brain and nervous system and sense organs is in the main *eliminative* and not productive. Each person is at each moment capable of remembering all that has ever happened to him and of perceiving everything that is happening everywhere in the universe. The function of the brain and nervous system is to protect us from being overwhelmed and confused by this mass of largely useless and irrelevant knowledge.[11]

Huxley then places Broad's view in the context of his own perennial philosophy, saying:

> According to such a theory, each one of us is potentially Mind at Large. But in so far as we are animals, our business is at all costs to survive. To make biological survival possible, Mind at Large has to be funneled through the reducing valve of the brain and nervous system. What comes out at the other end is a measly trickle.

When Huxley refers to the "Mind at Large," what he means is the divine ground, the Brahman. Even before his experiment with mescaline, Huxley had theorized that if somehow the reducing valve of the brain could be turned off, or, to put it another way, if the valve could be opened wider, then Mind at Large could enter and he himself might become Mind at Large. He hoped to achieve chemically what mystics had achieved through yoga, meditation, and other spiritual disciplines.

Huxley and Osmond believed that mescaline worked by inhibiting, in a non-dangerous way, the production of enzymes, which regulate the supply of glucose in the brain. Without the usual supply of sugar certain brain functions, including the tendency to process reality intellectually, would slow down. "When the brain runs out of sugar, the undernourished ego grows weak, can't be bothered to undertake the necessary chores . . . Mind at Large seeps past the no longer watertight valve."

This is what Aldous was hoping for, to experience Mind at Large and the reality "that All is in all—that All is actually each"—which he believed was as close as a finite mind could ever come to "perceiving everything that is happening everywhere in the universe." Simultaneous with this experience he hoped for a rest from his everyday sort of mind, including "the world of selves, of time, of moral judgements and utilitarian considerations, the world (and it was this aspect of human life which I wished, above all else, to forget) of self-assertion, of cocksureness, of overvalued words and idolatrously worshiped notions."[12]

The surprise for Aldous was that this actually seemed to happen. He became, to understate the matter, enraptured. In fact, it is not overstating the matter to say that it was one of the most personally significant experiences of his life. "I was seeing what Adam had seen on the morning of his creation—the miracle, moment by moment, of naked existence." On a tape recording made that day, Huxley repeated several times, "This is how one ought to see, how things really are." Huxley felt he had broken through into the kind of full-blown experiential truth he had sought since his days with D.H. Lawrence, though he now described it in the language of Vedanta. "The Beatific Vision, Sat Chit Ananda, Being-Awareness-Bliss—for the first time I understood, not on the verbal level, not by inchoate hints or at a distance, but precisely and completely what those prodigious syllables referred to."

Huxley found that he was actually experiencing "All is actually each," and was reminded of a Zen story about a novice monk who asks his master, "What is the Dharma-body of the Buddha?" To which the master answers, "The hedge at the bottom of the garden." Huxley interpreted this to mean that the Dharma-body of the Buddha is "anything that I—or rather the blessed Not-I, released for a moment from my throttling embrace—cared to look at. The books, for example, with which my study walls were lined . . . they glowed, when I looked at them, with brighter colors, a profounder significance."13

On some level Aldous's long-sought-after goal had been achieved. Certainly he had had glimpses of mystical experience before, but on mescaline he believed he was saturated with it. Brahman, oneness, was not a concept but a percept. He had transcended his ego, however briefly, and Mind at Large was looking out through his eyes.

In his novel *Island*, he later gave a description of this kind of experience:

> "Light," he whispered at last.
>
> "And you're there, looking at the light?"
>
> "Not looking at it," he answered, after a long reflective pause. "*Being* it. Being it," he repeated emphatically. . .
>
> *Its* presence was his absence. . . . Ultimately and essentially there was only a luminous bliss, only a knowledgeless understanding, only union with unity in a limitless, undifferentiated awareness. . . .
>
> Light here, light now. And because it was infinitely here and timelessly now, there was nobody outside the light to look at the light. The fact was the awareness, the awareness the fact.14

As the effects of the mescaline wore off that day, Huxley still found himself in a transfigured state that phenomenologically resembled, in his own mind at least, what the Vedantists described. However, and this is significant, Huxley also believed in retrospect that he had not experienced enlightenment. He had been given an experience of Mind at Large but that experience was, he believed, ultimately inferior to complete enlightenment in at least two important respects. First, because it was temporary. The experience lasted only a few hours and though it had a continuing inspirational value for him, its main import (the unitive awareness itself) could not be held onto. Second, Huxley felt that even within the experience itself a critical element of enlightenment had been missing, and that was the desire for altruistic behavior. During the session he mostly wanted to enjoy the depths of his own bliss and this disturbed him because, as Laura Huxley, his second wife, once pointed out, "In his later years Aldous put more and more emphasis on the danger of being addicted to meditation *only*, to knowledge *only*, to wisdom *only*—without love."

During the nineteen-forties Huxley had come to agree more with Buddhist categories describing the enlightened mind than those of Vedanta. Mahayana Buddhists specifically talk of the highest state of realization as that of the *bodhisattva*, who, unlike the Theravadin *arhat*, is not content merely to experience his or her own awakening but wishes to share their insight with others. As Huxley explains it:

> Over against the *arhat*, retreating from appearances into an entirely transcendental Nirvana, stands the Bodhisattva, for whom Suchness and the world of contingencies are one, and for whose boundless compassion every one of those contingencies is an occasion not only for transfiguring insight, but also for the most practical charity.[15]

Reflecting on the Arnold side of Aldous's nature it is not difficult to understand why this ideal appealed to him. Huxley agreed, as he often acknowledged, with Pascal who said, "The worship of truth without charity is idolatry." That first day he had lacked the will to care about others and consequently he believed that mescaline had helped him to know contemplation "at its height" but not in its "fullness." Enlightenment required one not only to experience the transcendental, the eternal, but also to be fully present in the imminent and the temporal, to connect with others as well as to be. Mescaline could be a part of the means to awakening, and Huxley would use it as such (once or twice a year), but it wasn't an end in itself.

> I am not so foolish as to equate what happens under the influence of mescalin or of any other drug, prepared or in the future preparable, with the realization of the end and ultimate purpose of human life: Enlightenment, the Beatific Vision. All I am suggesting is that the mescalin experience is what Catholic theologians call `a gratuitous grace,' not necessary to salvation but potentially helpful and to be accepted thankfully, if made available.[16]

It wasn't everything but it was something, and Huxley and Osmond were encouraged to try other experiments. After that first time Huxley wrote to Osmond, "What emerges as a general conclusion is the confirmation of the fact that mescalin does genuinely open the door . . ." Osmond was also pleased with the results—and pleased with Huxley, a first-class wordsmith who could describe the mescaline experience more lucidly than anyone had ever done before. This is significant in that it explains some of Huxley's impact on the next generation of spiritual seekers. Thus encouraged, Osmond proposed to the scientific community a less pejorative term for the class of drugs called "hallucinogens." With input from Huxley he suggested calling them "psychedelic," meaning "mind-opening," or "mind-revealing"—the term by which they're generally known today.

THE RESPONSE TO *The Doors of Perception* was anything but warm. Many critics were clearly outraged—some finding confirmation that Huxley had truly flipped his wig. According to David Dunaway in *Huxley in Hollywood,* "The bitterness triggered by Huxley's account of mescaline exceeded any previous criticisms he had received, even those of his pacifism. Huxley is 'bogged up neck-deep in his mystical dreams and fantasies,' opined The Indian Review."

"What people shied away from—or were attracted by," explains Sybille Bedford in her biography, "was the unfamiliarity, the way outness of the whole thing. Really Aldous was proving himself too amphibious by half; from enfant terrible of *Antic Hay* to psychedelic acolyte he had been slipping through everybody's net. Self-respecting rationalists saw fresh evidence of quackery and intellectual abdication while the serious and religious were bothered by the offer of a shortcut; but I rather think that the people who were most angry were the aesthetes who were really outraged by Aldous's attempt to put art in its place."[17]

Aldous did not believe he was thinking or acting irrationally. He was entertaining a rational hypothesis about a trans-rational experience. Furthermore, it wasn't counter-rational to say that a religious experience could be chemically conditioned. To defend this position he pointed out, "In one way or another, all our experiences are chemically conditioned, and if we imagine that some of them are purely 'spiritual,' purely 'intellectual,' purely 'aesthetic,' it is merely because we have never troubled to investigate the internal chemical environment at the moment of their occurrence."[18]

That Huxley was arguing for a shortcut, is both right and wrong. Earlier in his career he had indeed observed, many times, that the path to awakening was difficult. In the interview with Cyril Connolly in 1948 he had said, "Mystics have been found in every church, but unfortunately it is difficult to become one." When Aldous had said it was difficult "to become one" though, he didn't mean that it necessarily had to be. He was simply reporting the common experience and not disallowing the possibility of a faster route being found. Plus, he wasn't really changing his mind all that much from what he had told Connolly; since Huxley did not believe that mescaline experience is synonymous with enlightenment, just how short the shortcut would actually be remained to be seen.

Artists and aesthetes were appalled at Huxley's claim that true mystical experience seemed to make art obsolete. In *The Doors of Perception* he had written, "I strongly suspect that most of the great knowers of Suchness paid very little attention to art." And also, "Art, I suppose, is only for beginners, or else for those resolute dead-enders, who have made up their minds to be content with the ersatz of Suchness, with symbols rather than with what they signify, with the elegantly composed recipe in lieu of actual dinner."

Huxley was not criticizing artists themselves with these comments; in his book he had also said, "What the rest of us see only under the influence of mescalin, the artist is congenitally equipped to see all the time." Huxley's point was that for an enlightened person, whom he believed experienced every moment with consummate richness and significance, art, which he believed was only a means to that sweetness and light and not to be idolized in and of itself, would be no more valuable than "the hedge at the bottom of the garden." Huxley was in fact saying of art what Krishna had said of the Vedas, the sacred texts of Hinduism, in the *Bhagavad-Gita*:

> As much profit as there is in a well
> When on all sides there is a flood of water,
> No more value is there in all the Vedas
> For the one who is enlightened.[19]

Huxley wasn't saying that art is uniformly worthless. He was saying that it is of much less value for someone who has become a living Buddha. That his position constitutes much of a threat to museums and galleries seems doubtful as most people are likely to fall short of that mark and could, after all, use the boost toward realization that Huxley believed art can give. It's interesting though what Huxley reveals about his esthetic theory. Ultimately, art is not a class of objects for Huxley, it is an experience that objects can solicit—if they are constructed with genius and if their viewers are sophisticated enough to appreciate them. In *Heaven and Hell*, another short book based on his psychedelic experiences published in 1956, he praises several artists for their ability to create vehicles leading to visionary and mystical experience, e.g., Rembrandt, Vuillard, and Paolo Uccello—whose stained-glass window of the Resurrection Huxley says is "perhaps the most extraordinary single work of vision-inducing art ever produced." In the end Huxley was only saying something like this: "I think that I shall never see a poem as lovely as a tree," in that the human mind, if properly awake, could see all the world as a continuous masterpiece of unsurpassed beauty and not require humanly created art for its edification.

IN THE SPRING AND SUMMER of 1954 Aldous and Maria took a tour of the Middle East, Egypt, and Greece and then stopped off in Western Europe on their way back home to California. It had become clear to Maria that her condition was getting worse. Upon seeing her doctor in Paris, she was advised to return to her own doctors in America as soon as possible. Aldous, still unaware of the severity of her illness, and believing the cancer was cured, was disappointed about cutting the trip short. Soon after his sixtieth birthday they left for home. During that fall Maria's condition fluctuated but always the overall direction was downward. Aldous traveled to keep up with his lecture commitments and Maria received regular treatments for her cancer. In February of 1955 it was undeniable that she was not going to recover.

Aldous spent many days simply sitting beside her bed, sometimes speaking and sometimes just sitting quietly. When he did speak he usually gave "suggestions about her physical well-being," using the power of suggestion to calm her and to help ease her pain. When it was obvious that she was dying these suggestions increased. More than a year before, during Aldous's first mescaline experience, he had contemplated how difficult it would be for him to stay centered if he were to become frightened. "Would you be able," Maria had asked, "to fix your attention on what *The Tibetan Book of the Dead* calls the Clear Light?" Aldous was doubtful but remarked, "Perhaps I could— but only if there were somebody there to tell me about the Clear Light." In the days and hours leading up to Maria's death, Aldous was there to remind her about the Clear Light.

On February 12, as she was failing, Aldous began a careful and loving description of images to her—many of them drawn from their time in the desert at Llano, which Maria had particularly loved.

"And I would ask her to look at these lights of her beloved     desert and to realize that they were not merely symbols, but actual expression of the divine nature; an expression of Pure Being, an expression of the peace that passeth all understanding; an expression of the divine joy; an expression of the love which is at the heart of things, at the core, along with peace and joy and being, of every human mind. . . .

"I told her to let go, to forget the body, to leave it lying here like a bundle of old clothes and to allow herself to he carried, as a child is carried, into the heart of the rosy light of love. She knew what love was, had been capable of love as few human beings are capable. Now she must go forward into love, must permit herself to be carried into love, deeper and deeper into it, so that at last she would be capable of loving as God loves—of loving everything, infinitely, without judging, without condemning, without either craving or abhorring." And then there was peace:

> Go forward into the light. Let yourself be carried into light. No memories, no regrets, no looking backwards, no apprehensive thoughts about your own or anyone else's future. Only light. Only this pure being, this love, this joy. Above all this peace. Peace in this timeless moment, peace now, peace now.[20]

Matthew, who had recently completed a master's degree in public health from Harvard, had flown out to California to be with his parents. In a 1985 interview with Dunaway, Matthew described what happened that day: "Those last three hours were the most anguishing and moving of my life. . . Aldous was whispering to her the lesson of *The Tibetan Book of the Dead* . . but framed in such a moving and personal way . . . illustrations of their life together. . . . It was over so quietly and gently with Aldous with tears streaming down his face with his quiet voice not breaking."

Finally the end came, though Aldous reflected thankfully that when "the breathing ceased, at about six, it was without any struggle." Maria Huxley was fifty-seven years old. *The Doors of Perception*, Aldous's last book published before her death, was dedicated to her.

# - 10 -

# DRIVE-IN WEDDING CHAPEL

*"God is love." What manifest nonsense, and yet it happens to be true.*
—A character from Huxley's *Island*

IN AGREEMENT WITH Maria's philosophy Huxley, too, sought to keep himself present after her death and not wallow in sadness. But it was difficult for him emotionally—as it was physically, since he now had to do most things for himself. He said that he felt "amputated," and repeated this comment many times to many friends. He had been with Maria for more than thirty-five years and though she often dismissed herself as not being his equal, Aldous adored her and trusted her judgment about his books, and about life itself. He once wrote, "In so far as I learned to be human—and I had a great capacity for not being human—it is thanks to her."[1]

Aldous did his best to get on with things and 1955 became an important year in his life for many reasons. It was at this time that he began a two-year stint of writing articles, on whatever he wished, for *Esquire* magazine. This helped his ideas to reach a wider audience and supplied him with the steady income he had been missing ever since work in the movies had dried up. Also in 1955 *The London Magazine* sponsored a critical symposium on Huxley's writings. The symposium, which Huxley did not attend, focused on his novels specifically. The event highlights a tendency, both then and now, to deal with Aldous mainly as a novelist—an ironic tendency in that so few of his books were novels and in that his primary contribution to the human search for meaning arguably came in other areas.

However, his novels were certainly influential and—despite his pro-testations to the contrary—several were critical successes that remain important works today.

During the spring of that year Aldous also began spending time with Laura Archera, a friend of his and Maria. Archera, born and raised in Italy, had become a concert violinist who debuted at Carnegie Hall and later worked in filmmaking. Finally, she had become a therapist. Aldous and Maria had first met her in 1948, when she had approached Aldous to write a script for a film she hoped to make about the famous *Palio* horse race in Italy. Huxley was interested but Archera was not able to find funding and the project finally collapsed. Huxley and Archera met again in 1952, at a dinner party, but no close relationship occurred until the summer of 1953. Archera was then living in Rome and the Huxleys, traveling in Europe at the time, visited her. The three became close and, despite Maria's weakening condition, took excursions together to see the sights. Once back in Los Angeles that fall, the friendship continued, and after Maria's death Laura was one of those who checked in on Aldous regularly to make sure he was managing. Aldous spent the summer of 1955 in Connecticut, visiting Matthew and his family, which now included a daughter, Tess; but that fall his relationship with Laura deepened and in March of 1956, they were married.

The summer before Aldous had been driven East by his sister-in-law, Rose. While passing through Yuma, Arizona, he had been intrigued by a drive-in wedding chapel they had passed. After proposing to Archera that next winter, Huxley added, "Do you think it might be amusing to drive to Yuma and get married at the drive-in?" Laura later wrote about her reaction, "Nothing could delight me more, I said. I have an anti-ritualistic streak in me, and a 'drive-in marriage' was most unritualistically attractive."[2] (The circumstances of the wedding, described in detail in her book, *This Timeless Moment*, are an engrossing read.) Huxley, in so many ways the consummate iconoclast, simultaneously embraced the experience as serious and wonderfully absurd—Thomas Huxley, one imagines, would have approved. But the wedding had its troubled moment. Huxley later wrote to his son, Matthew, that, "two minutes after signing the license," he had felt a twinge of being unfaithful to Maria's memory, but then the cloud passed. "Tenderness, I discovered, is the best memorial to tenderness."

That summer, just before his sixty-second birthday, Aldous and Laura moved out of Kings Road and into a new house in the Hollywood Hills. Soon Huxley would publish *Adonis and the Alphabet* (released in the United States as *Tomorrow and Tomorrow and Tomorrow*), based around his articles for *Esquire* and including details of his theory of how best to educate a human being, the "multiple amphibian." In the book he explains many of the ideas on education he had worked out in conversations with Krishnamurti. Although in the late nineteen-fifties Huxley actually published very little; significantly, though, in addition to *Adonis and the Alphabet*, he wrote a series of articles commissioned by the Long Island tabloid *Newsday*. His specific project was to appraise how near or far he believed society had moved toward the dystopia he had described in *Brave New World*. The insightful articles were collected and published in 1958 as *Brave New World Revisited*.

Huxley begins the book by stating, "The prophecies I made in 1931 are coming true much sooner than I thought they would," and so sets the tone of his explanations. He tells us that the centralization of political and economic power which would be necessary to the formation of a World State was clearly increasing, and that the pressing problem of over-population threatened to push it further, "Over-population leads to economic insecurity and social unrest. Unrest and insecurity lead to more control by central governments and an increase of their power." Furthermore, over-organization, nationalization, and mechanization were turning people into "automata" and the "likeness of termites." Huxley had read Hitler's *Mein Kampf* out-lining his racial theories, domestic policies, methods of mind control, and plans for world conquest, and Huxley used the dictator's words as a warning against thinking as a mob, a possibility he clearly loathed.

> In a word, a man in a crowd behaves as though he
> had swallowed a large dose of some powerful intox-
> icant. He is a victim of what I have called 'herd-

poisoning.' Like alcohol, herd-poison is an active, extroverted drug. The crowd-intoxicated individual escapes from responsibility, intelligence and morality into a kind of frantic, animal mindlessness.

Several chapters deal directly with propaganda and brainwashing. In them Huxley argued that we must be on guard to prevent herd-intoxication. We must learn to think clearly and how not to be drawn in by overly emotional or otherwise vacuous pronouncements in the media. After the Russians put the first satellite into orbit many were referring to the modern epoch as the "Space Age," but Huxley thought it would be better named the "Age of Over-population," or the "Age of Television Addiction."

> Children as might be expected, are highly susceptible to propaganda. They are ignorant of the world and its ways, and therefore completely unsuspecting. Their critical faculties are undeveloped. The youngest of them have not yet reached the age of reason and the older ones lack the experience on which their new-found rationality can effectively work. In Europe, conscripts used to be playfully referred to as "cannon fodder." Their little brothers and sisters have now become radio fodder and television fodder.

To combat the forces urging us toward the World State, Aldous advocated that we educate ourselves. "The effects of false and pernicious propaganda cannot be neutralized except by a thorough training in the art of analyzing its techniques and seeing through its sophistries." He said we must do whatever possible to create a truly free press, rather than the advertisement-driven media we now have, for a better—less entertainment oriented—presentation of issues. He also advocated campaign reform for politicians, including ceilings on campaign spending. He advised that we must also guard against becoming too complacent or too numb—that rather than medicating ourselves with tranquilizers (which he equates with the soma of *Brave New World*) to deal with the stress of our life, we should question that life itself. Finally, he said we must empower ourselves as individuals to become activists for these causes. We may feel helpless and insignificant but we must remember that we are not.

> In real life, life as it is lived from day to day, the individual can never be explained away. It is only in theory that his contributions appear to approach zero; in practice they are all-important. When a piece of work gets done in the world, who actually does it? Whose eyes and ears do the perceiving, whose cortex does the thinking, who has the feelings that motivate, the will that overcomes obstacles? Certainly not the social environment; for a group is not an organism, but only a blind unconscious organization. Everything that is done within a society is done by individuals.

Early in the book Huxley had stated what he believed was essential: "That we are being propelled in the direction of *Brave New World* is obvious. But no less obvious is the fact that we can, if we so desire, refuse to co-operate."

HUXLEY'S MARRIAGE WITH Laura Archera was different from his marriage with Maria. Laura was, and remained until her death in 2007, a free spirit, and Aldous was left more to fend for himself. But Aldous seems to have enjoyed this arrangement, reveling in his own freedom to move around and make schedules at will. His time was being in creasingly taken up with speaking engagements all across the country and plans were easier to make if he traveled alone; Laura rarely went out on the road with him. However, in 1958, when they were invited to visit Brazil at the request of its president, she went along to support him. Once in South America Huxley realized that his fame had spread below the equator. When he and Laura reached

Above:
Krishnamurti lecturing to group in Pennsylvania.

(Public Domain, National Archives)

Below: Krishnamurti *(far right)*    (National Archives)

San Paolo the newspaper announced in banner headlines, "HUXLEY ARRIVES!" And when they stayed in Rio de Janeiro, a daily column referred to Aldous as *O Sabio*, "The Sage." He found the reference both flattering and comical.

Huxley continued this unplanned victory tour that October in England. The reason for his visit seems largely to have been to congratulate his brother in person for having been recently knighted. In 1953 Julian had won the Darwin Medal of the Royal Society for his work in evolutionary biology, and in 1954 he had received the Darwin-Wallace Commemorative Medal of the Linnean Society. These honors combined with his prestige as a public personality and regular voice on the BBC had led to his knighthood. Laura Huxley relates that Aldous, too, had been nominated for the honor but, not wishing to steal any of his brother's glory, wrote a letter to the queen politely declining.

In England, where he was still a citizen (he had been denied U.S. citizenship in 1953 because of his pacifism—or, more accurately, for not being willing to label his pacifism a *religious* consideration), Huxley had an opportunity to catch up with old friends and to be interviewed by the press. He was happy to reunite with T.S. Eliot, but now found him to be "curiously dull—as a result perhaps of being, at last, happy in his second marriage." And old friends had a chance to catch up with the new, transfigured Aldous. "It was around this time that Aldous developed a radiance," his nephew Francis remarked. "You felt in his presence something—extraordinary."[3] Or as Ronald Clark summed it up: "Within these few years after his second marriage it did seem as though, in Frieda Lawrence's words, something 'had burst forth out of him.' It was almost as if a new awareness of what he had been trying to say all his life had suddenly been born within him."[4]

Aldous was older now, and with age his tendency to grizzle had lessened. Where once he had felt pleased with his acid tongue and justified in his pontifications, he now spoke mostly out of compassion. Where once he had made what seem today preposterous judgments about other cultures, Aldous's tone is significantly changed in his later works. (In 1923, he opened an article called "Tibet," with the statement, "In moments of complete despair, when it seems that all is for the worst in the worst of all possible worlds, it is cheering to discover that there are places where stupidity reigns even more despotically than in Western Europe." And in *Jesting Pilate,* published in 1926, which describes his first trip to India, he had said, "It seems to me that any one who professes an ardent admiration for the Taj Mahal must look at it without having any standards of excellence in his mind.") Aldous now more fully recognized his tendency to judge and left it behind. In this regard, a letter he wrote to his son in 1959 is significant. Matthew was going through a divorce and Aldous, saddened by the situation, urged him to be compassionate toward Ellen, his wife:

> Huxleys especially have a tendency not to suffer fools gladly—and also to regard as fools people who are merely different from themselves in temperament and habits. It is difficult for Huxleys to remember that other people have as much right to their habits and temperaments as Huxleys have to theirs. . . So do remember this family vice of too much judging.[5]

In reading Huxley's letters today it seems he felt an urgency as he aged. He wished deeply to be of service to humanity and never seemed to feel he had done enough. In *Brave New World Revisited* he had pointed out that "nothing short of everything is ever really enough." And so he kept up his travels and kept up his lecturing, offering his diverse solutions to those forces that would limit our freedoms and standardize our thinking. The ironically amused Pyrrhonic esthete had now fully become the engaged intellectual activist.

IN 1959 HUXLEY WAS, for two semesters (spring and fall) a visiting professor at the University of California at Santa Barbara (these lectures were posthumously published as *The Human Situation*). His reputation as a speaker, no less than his reputation as an intellectual had brought this about. Of course, there's a bit of irony here in that Huxley had always hated public speaking, but Laura Huxley later shed light on what had led him to accept the posts: "Aldous told me he had not always been so calm about lecturing. 'What changed you?' He laughed. 'I only had to realize that I wasn't as important as all that!'"

In May Aldous received two great honors, his first honorary Ph.D., from UCSB, and the Award of Merit for the Novel from the American Academy of Arts and Letters. The honors touched him deeply, if only because they indicated there was respect for progressive ideas, ideas that could help fulfill the individual and move society toward humanism and sustainability.

His experiments with psychedelic drugs continued and had grown to include a couple of experiences with LSD—but publicly Aldous was staying fairly quiet on the subject. The next fall he would mention these substances in his classes at UCSB, and he would publish an article on psychedelics in *The Saturday Evening Post* called, "Drugs That Shape Men's Minds," but for the most part he contained his enthusiasm. Ever since the backlash over *The Doors of Perception* in 1955 he had coaxed Osmond and others also to proceed slowly and carefully.

In 1956 he wrote to Osmond about why he didn't want to be on television talking about psychedelics even though he had been asked:

> Mescalin, it seems to me, and the odder aspects of mind are matters to be written about for a small public, not discussed on TV in the presence of a vast audience of Baptists, Methodists and nothing-but-men plus an immense lunatic fringe. . . . As you say . . . we still know very little about the psychedelics, and, until we know a good deal more, I think the matter should be discussed . . . in the relative privacy of learned journals, the decent obscurity of moderately highbrow books and articles. What one says on the air is bound to be misunderstood.[6]

Huxley personally had no doubt psychedelics, if approached correctly and responsibly, could provide meaningful experience. He himself had had a meaningful experience, and as a longtime advocate of experiential truth he saw no reason to doubt it. Something beneficial had come his way. ("The cultured melancholy resignation of Matthew Arnold, which I ordinarily like and feel at home with, is felt under LSD to be far too negative—unrealistically so.") However, he also understood that not everyone would use these substances responsibly. Then, too, he appreciated that experimentation with them had only just begun and that even favorable theories about psychedelics were, after all, only theories, which must be explored further before full advocacy could be given. In fact, he respected Osmond because he wasn't too attached to any particular theory of what was happening in the psychedelic experience. "You unquestionably *are* the man to act as liaison officer between pure science and the rest of the world in this matter," he wrote, adding:

> [__]could not possibly do it. He is able and he is likeable; but he has not yet reached affective and intellectual maturity. He is obsessed with his ideas— rides them like hobby-horses and is ridden by them, so that there is in him a certain lack of flexibility, a certain one-trackedness which would be an insurmountable obstacle in performing the necessary task.[7]

When appraising why it was best to go slowly, Huxley worried that serious research could be undermined by those who wished only to find a new thrill. In this regard, he answered a letter from Thomas Merton, the poet and Trappist monk, who was interested in Huxley's opinion about psychedelics, that "the experience is so transcendentally important that it is in no circumstances a thing to be entered upon light-heartedly or for enjoyment."

But Huxley was having trouble keeping the lid on. One reason was Gerald Heard. Trabuco College had failed in 1949 and by 1951

Heard was fully back in Huxley's life. This was a happy occurrence for Aldous. Heard was less driven and puritanical than he had been before and Huxley enjoyed having someone of a like mind to talk with. When Huxley became involved with mescaline he shared his thoughts with Heard, and then he shared mescaline also. Heard, always enthusiastic about what he believed, became almost instantly a great advocate for psychedelic experience and spread the news to his fans, a group who called themselves the "Wayfarers" and who published a newsletter.

According to Dr. Oscar Janiger, Heard heralded psychedelics as the "first hint of the oncoming Psychological Revolution, the Copernican Revolution of and in the Mind." Janiger, a psychologist who became famous for LSD research and therapy (and who later, according to Timothy Leary, turned-on Cary Grant, Jack Nicholson, and others) had learned about LSD from Heard in 1954 and later explained: "He told me that the emergence of LSD in the twentieth century was simply God's way of giving us the gift of consciousness. He believed that LSD was a device for saving humanity from Armageddon."[8]

It was becoming increasingly difficult for Aldous to contain Heard and those others who had accepted Huxley's own interpretation of the significance of the drug experience. People were taking Huxley's lead whether he liked it or not. He had, in fact, set off a brush fire. "We were the only group, to my knowledge," Janiger later related of his Los Angeles friends, "that was really beginning to study this 'mystical'—if you will, 'transcendental'—aspect of it. . . . It's just that the medicine fell on some far more profound people here than it did elsewhere, I can assure you. That was what did it. It fell on Huxley and Heard." Aldous could not have anticipated where that accidental brush fire would spread. Soon, posthumously, he would be a counterculture hero, his small book becoming the inspiration for the name of Jim Morrison's band, The Doors, and Huxley himself one of the faces on the 1967 cover of The Beatles' *Sgt. Pepper's* record album. As Dunaway writes in *Huxley in Hollywood*, "Huxley unwittingly set in motion an international movement of drug experimentation involving millions of American and European youths; not accidentally did

Timothy Leary and Richard Alpert later dedicate their adaptation of the *Bardo Thodol, The Psychedelic Experience*, to Aldous Huxley."[9]

# - 11 -

## TIMOTHY LEARY

*In brief, the really possible Utopia would be this world
experienced by a psychophysique at full aperture.*
—Gerald Heard

WHEN HUXLEY ARRIVED at MIT in the fall of 1960 he was riding a wave of interest in his work. His visiting professorship at the
Menninger Foundation that spring had been a success (some of the
material from those lectures appears in his last book, *Literature and
Science*) and he had just been nominated for the Nobel Prize for literature. In the end he didn't win the Nobel but he took the loss in
stride. "Aldous's freedom was not only intellectual," Laura Huxley
once explained, "it was the emotional freedom from possessiveness,
from the need of being a winner." In fact, Huxley actually found it
difficult to take himself seriously as a great man, once telling Humph-
rey Osmond that he "was uncomfortable being eulogized because he
either felt like laughing or looking around to get a glimpse of the ad-
mirable person for whom the nice speeches were being made." (Huxley's non-attachment aside, one must wonder if his chances for the
Nobel Prize wouldn't have been better if he hadn't constantly
claimed that he wasn't really a novelist.)

Among those eager to meet Aldous while he was in Cambridge
was a young psychologist from Harvard who had recently gained the
respect of his peers for his book *Interpersonal Diagnosis of Personality.*
His name was Timothy Leary, and along with several of his col-
leagues (including Richard Alpert, Ralph Metzner, and Gunther

Weil), he was beginning a research project to outline the effects and possible benefits of psilocybin, a synthesized form of the psychedelic substance in the *psilcybe cubensis* mushroom. Leary was aware of Huxley's books on mind-opening drugs and decided to write him a letter explaining his research plans and inviting Huxley to comment or participate. Aldous gave Leary a call back and so began an infamous chain of events.

Leary came to MIT (which he often jokingly pointed out is TIM spelled backwards) to pick up Huxley and the two went off to the Harvard Faculty Club for lunch. According to Leary, Huxley studied the menu with a magnifying glass "as though it were a scientific specimen," and then said, "It seems to be pre-ordained that we order the soup." Leary asked what kind it was. Huxley burst into laughter and replied, "Mushroom."

They had a long meeting during which each seems to have impressed the other. Leary says in his autobiography that they met several more times that fall and that when his first shipment of psilocybin arrived, just before Thanksgiving, he and Huxley took some together. "For the next three hours we listened to music—Bach, Mozart, African drums, Indian chants, Ravi Shankar." Then they began talking about how to "introduce these methods of mind expansion to society." Leary relates that Huxley advised him to keep their findings private. To study them scientifically, and in the meantime also to initiate such artists and intellectuals as seemed safe and appropriate. Leary disagreed with this approach, arguing that society needed the "information" held in psychedelics and balked at what he perceived to be Huxley's elitism. Huxley reminded Leary that a few mistakes could cause suppression of psychedelics and that substance prohibitions went back as far in time as the Garden of Eden.

Leary was quiescent for a few months but increasingly came to believe, as did Heard, that psychedelics were the answer and that the answer should not be suppressed. He felt Huxley had stumbled onto something amazing—"I believe that no one over fifty can quite realize how exciting Huxley seems to the generation which followed their own." Leary was increasingly seeing psychedelics as a panacea—and even as late as 1968 wrote that LSD specifically was "exactly the right answer for the particular neurological disease that man has been plagued by for the last thousand years."

Aldous did not see it as a panacea, and, in fact, he didn't believe in panaceas. Human life is too complex he argued in his last novel, *Island*, for there to be only one answer. Psychedelics were simply one tool, and a tool that could easily be misused. However, Leary's excitement was difficult to contain. He and Alpert, his lead research partner, began sharing drugs with their undergraduate students and Leary, following Huxley's advice, also "initiated" artists—including Allen Ginsberg and Jack Kerouac. Ginsberg, who also had an interest in Asian mysticism, became especially enthused by his psychedelic experience and urged Leary not to listen to Huxley—to go public. Leary agreed and began dispensing psilocybin and LSD openly, which led to his dismissal from Harvard in 1962. Alpert, who would soon travel to India, and eventually become the spiritual teacher known today as Ram Dass, was also fired. With Alpert's help, Leary then became the Johnny Appleseed of psychedelics, publishing books and giving lectures all over the country about his new psychedelic religion. One consequence of this was that college kids throughout America were soon reading *The Doors of Perception*.

Another figure important in the psychedelic revolution was Huxley's longtime friend Alan Watts. Watts is important here not only because he endorsed the use of psychedelics but because he helped popularize Huxley's interpretation of the experience. Watts was born in England in 1915, held an M.A. in theology, and had spent a brief but intense period as an Episcopalian priest. Finding that he didn't like the priesthood he moved to California around 1950. In 1955 he became the dean of the American Academy of Asian Studies and worked closely with D.T. Suzuki and Christmas Humphreys—the two most important figures teaching the Western world about Buddhism at that time. Watts eventually became a friend of Jack Kerouac, Gary Snyder, and other of the Beat artists but long before that, in 1942, he formed a relationship with Huxley.

Watts had first written to Aldous about his book *Grey Eminence* in which Watts initially learned of the writings of Saint Dionysius, a Christian mystic. In Watts' own next book, *Behold the Spirit*, published in 1947, which was a critique of formal Christianity's failure to recognize and include mysticism as a living part of its teachings, he borrows heavily from Huxley's ideas. The two men first met in person in New York in 1943, and Aldous, reinforcing Watts' interest in Asian religions, recommended that he also investigate the Vedanta teachings. Watts began studying Vedanta as well as Buddhism, and in 1966 wrote one of the most readable short introductions to Vedanta ever published, titled simply *The Book*. In the late 1950s, Watts also became interested in psychedelics and explored them for himself. For a time he was nearly as enthusiastic about them as Leary (to whom he had been introduced by Huxley), and the two men collaborated in 1962 on a book lauding psychedelic mysticism, called *The Joyous Cosmology*. Watts knew Aldous did not want to popularize psychedelics; howver, he finally decided that "Aldous had already let the cat out of the bag in The *Doors of Perception* and *Heaven and Hell*," and felt he might as well express his own opinion.

In *The Joyous Cosmology* Watts agrees with Huxley that LSD and other such drugs are only a tool and not a panacea but they *are* a tool and should not be dismissed or suppressed. In the text, he and Leary both reinforced Aldous's interpretation of psychedelic experience in Asian mystical terms. To some extent this bothered Aldous in that it boosted the association between his name and LSD in the public's awareness and it wasn't moving cautiously. In December of 1962 he wrote to Osmond to complain about Leary in particular:

> I spent an evening with him here a few weeks ago—
> and he talked such nonsense . . . that I became quite
> concerned. Not about his sanity—because he is per-
> fectly sane—but about his prospects in the world;
> for this nonsense—talking is just another device for
> annoying people in authority, flouting convention,
> cocking snooks at the academic world. It is the reac-
> tion of a mischievous Irish boy to the headmaster of
> his school. . . . I am very fond of Tim—but why, oh
> why, does he have to be such an ass? I have told
> him repeatedly that the only attitude for a researcher

in this ticklish field is that of an anthropologist living in the midst of a tribe of potentially dangerous savages. Go about your business quietly, don't break the taboos or criticize the locally accepted dogmas... If you leave them alone they'll probably leave you alone.[1]

But Leary wasn't going to leave anyone alone. In fact, by the time Huxley wrote his letter to Osmond, Leary had already shifted into high gear. The previous spring he had participated in a research project that he interpreted as the first step in the scientific confirmation of psychedelic mysticism. The project was run by Dr. Walter Pahnke, a medical doctor who was studying for his doctoral degree in the philosophy of religion at Harvard. Pahnke's project was an attempt to establish whether or not there is any resemblance between psychedelic experience and the "spontaneous" experiences of mystics. Pahnke relied on a typology of mystical experience first compiled by the respected scholar of mysticism, W. T. Stace. Stace had analyzed a multitude of experiences from mystics of several cultures and determined that they were generally characterized by nine features: unity, transcendence of time and space, a deeply felt positive mood, a sense of sacredness, a noetic quality of extreme reality, paradoxicality, ineffability, transiency, and a persisting sense of positive influence after the experience.

The project involved twenty-four participants (with Leary absent), of which half were given psilocybin and half a placebo. Pahnke concluded, to many psychologists' surprise, that, "those subjects who received psilocybin experienced phenomena which were indistinguishable from if not identical with . . . the categories defined by our typology of mysticism." Leary was ecstatic, and later wrote in his autobiography that Pahnke's study "provided a scientific demonstration that spiritual ecstasy, religious revelation, and union with God were now directly accessible."

Of course, one study does not constitute scientific proof (and neither did Pahnke's study confirm Huxley's Vedantic and Buddhistic interpretation of the psychedelic experience) but Leary himself was convinced and spread the word with greater fervor.

The strongest and most complex arguments against psychedelic mysticism initially came from R.C. Zaehner, an Oxford professor and respected expert on Oriental mysticism, who specifically criticized the notion that chemicals could illicit a genuine mystical experience. He argued that Huxley's position was "both incoherent and self-contradictory," and that true transfiguration required an intimacy with a personal God (which, of course, as Huxley later pointed out, is highly debatable). He also argued, more cogently, that Huxley's experiences on mescaline had corresponded very closely with the experiences he had lovingly described in his previous writings—and so perhaps wish fulfillment was involved. Was it true mystical experience or not? This became a heated debate and the debate, in fact, continues today.

In light of contemporary knowledge, specifically the ethnographies of myriad cultures, in looking back on this debate, what strikes one first is the immense cultural myopia surrounding it. Whether such things as transfigured states of consciousness really exist is difficult to say, but that psychoactive substances can create such experiences as those we *call* transfigured seems beyond dispute. That is, since many, many world cultures have included psychedelically induced mysticism into their religions (and, with reference to mescaline itself, the religion of the Huichol Indians of northern Mexico is a good example), to dismiss psychedelic mysticism as invalid is clearly intellectually pretentious and culturally snobbish. However, Zaehner's point remains an important one. Huxley interpreted his experience largely in terms of Hindu and Buddhist categories that do not in many cases correlate with how psychedelic experience is interpreted in most psychedelic religions—including that of the Huichol. Transfiguration seems certain; whether that experience is really significant and how its significance is to be interpreted are the issues still alive today.


AFTER MIT, HUXLEY CONTINUED giving lectures around the country and would, the next year, start another visiting professorship at Berkeley. Meanwhile he was working on a novel—a very different kind of novel than any he had written before. He was describing a fictitious society that employed his many recommendations for advancing civilization—a society living closer to our true potential and pointing in the direction of new possibilities.

One evening in May of 1961, he was finishing the new novel at home in the Hollywood Hills when a fire broke out. It had been a hot, dry day in a series of like days. Laura was away from the house, but eventually came rushing in to tell him that the hills were on fire. Aldous jumped up and together they moved their car out of danger and then returned home to pack up and save what they could. Unfortunately, the brush was burning quickly, fanned by a breeze, and there was very little time to do anything. Aldous grabbed the manuscript for his utopian novel and Laura grabbed her violin, a 256-year-old Guarnieri. Little else was rescued. The house, along with many others, burned to the ground, taking with it Aldous's library of four thousand volumes plus an original copy of *Candide* inherited from Thomas Henry Huxley, the original manuscript of Lawrence's novel *St. Mawr*, letters and books signed by famous friends, and a chest containing his letters to Maria—the best source of information about his own life. "I am now a man without possessions and without a past," he wrote to his son Matthew the next day. And to a friend he added, "I am evidently intended to learn a little in advance of the final denudation, that you can't take it with you."

After the fire Laura moved in with her friend Ginny Pfeiffer, and Huxley moved into Gerald Heard's house for a while. It was at Heard's that he finished the new novel, *Island*, in June of 1961. The novel is set on the fictitious tropical island of Pala, somewhere southeast of India, where a group of visionaries have created a society without vulgarity, idolatry, materialism, or oppression of the individual. Where humans live in harmony with nature and where technology is subordinated to the health of all species. In the novel Huxley ground his axe about "progress" largely being an illusion. "Technology accelerates our progress but this is often only a progress toward acceleration," explains a character in Oliver Hockenhill's film about Huxley, *The Gravity of Light*.[2]

On Pala progress is measured in broader and more humane terms: as spiritual growth for the individual and as social and ecological harmony. Industry and industriousness are not considered sacred in and of themselves. For instance, Will Farnaby, the outsider who acts as the reader's guide to Pala, asks about the Palanese custom of avoiding strict specialization in their work force:

> "Does that kind of part-time system work well?"
> "It depends what you mean by 'well.' It doesn't result in maximum efficiency. But then in Pala maximum efficiency isn't the categorical imperative that it is with you. . . . If it's a choice between mechanical efficiency and human satisfaction, we choose satisfaction."

To design his Palanese society Huxley drew on many sources. "Greek history, Polynesian anthropology, translations from Sanskrit and Chinese Buddhist texts, scientific papers on pharmacology, neuro-physiology, psychology and education, together with novels, poems, critical essays, travel books, political commentaries and conversations with all kinds of people .. . everything went into the hopper." We find the Palanese employ such things as hypnosis, the Sheldonian personality typology, the Alexander techniques of physical reeducation, the Bates Method for training the eyes, and a variety of yoga and meditation exercises from Asian religions.

Like Huxley, the founders of Pala hoped to make the best of Western scientific culture, including its theoretical vanguard, as well as Asian mystical insights. Socially the Palanese are egalitarian and politically they are democratic—with a nominal royalty who unfortunately wish to be more powerful, to the eventual detriment of Pala. The Palanese focus their lives on finding spiritual happiness in the here and now, and to help them do so Mynar birds fly about and are trained to say, "Attention," like Zen masters calling their students into the present. "Attention" is the first and last word in Palanese society; it is also literally the first and last word in Huxley's last novel. The Palanese also make use of psychedelics. Unlike the soma drug in

*Brave New World*, the psychedelic substance on Pala is used sparingly and with reverence. It is not for clouding the mind or placating it with pleasure but rather for opening it up to the world. Called "moksha-medicine," the drug is for "liberation." Liberation not only for the individual but *through* the individual for society also. In *Island*, Huxley expresses his mature viewpoint on mind-opening drugs, what Laura Huxley once called, "the social meaning of the psychedelic experience." Exactly what that meaning was is summarized in a comment Aldous once made in a letter to Albert Hofmann, the Swiss chemist who first created LSD. Huxley had met Hofmann in Zurich in August of 1961 and learned that Hoffman was a fan of his. The feeling was mutual and when *Island* came out in the spring of 1962, Aldous sent him a copy inscribed, "To Dr. Albert Hofmann, the original discoverer of the moksha medicine." Along with the book he included a letter in which he articulated the highest value of all mystical insight:

> Meister Eckhart wrote that "what is taken in by contemplation must be given out in love." Essentially this is what must be developed—the art of giving out in love and intelligence what is taken in from vision and the experience of self-transcendence and solidarity with the Universe.[3]

When *Island* was released Cyril Connolly said it was Huxley's most important novel since *Time Must Have a Stop*, published in 1944, and few critics argued with him—but that didn't mean that they liked it. In fact, most critics did not. Some reproved the shallowness of the plot (which Huxley himself admitted was weak. When he had been writing the novel he had asked Christopher Isherwood to help fix what he called "the low ratio of story to exposition."). Others weighed the novel for irony and satire, Huxley's usual strengths, and found it lacking. Sybille Bedford, in her biography, explains: "To a great many, the book was a boring tale of preaching goody-goodies."

Huxley attributed the critics' acerbity to the fact that there is less pathos in happiness and he wrote to his niece: "It's with bad sentiments that one makes good novels. Which is why, as a novel, *Island* is so inadequate." But. Huxley had been trying to do something else with this book; he had been attempting to make a good society rather than a good novel, and he was hurt by the wholesale dismissal of his propositions. Huxley wondered if people weren't so tied to their cynicism that they couldn't allow for a constructive proposal. In the *Memorial Volume* to Aldous Huxley published after his death, Heard said that Huxley felt a reversal had taken place in society and that now to bare one's soul would awaken as much revulsion as if one had bared one's body in an earlier epoch.

Certainly Aldous was disappointed by the critical reaction to *Island,* but it is doubtful that he was surprised. He knew most people supposed they had better things to do then entertain utopian fantasies. The irony for him was that he believed that much of what prevented the "fantasies" from coming true was the misperception that they were fantasies. He thought he was pragmatic in his recommendations and, in fact, began the novel with a quote from Aristotle: "In framing an ideal we may assume what we wish, but should avoid impossibilities." However, his own cynicism coached him not to suppose he would be taken seriously. Perhaps this is why Huxley ended his novel with the island of Pala being overrun by military forces eager to exploit the island's oil wealth. Huxley warns us that the goodness of an idea does not protect it from harm and that if we really want positive change we must work diligently for it.

Despite the critical failure of *Island,* it nonetheless went into many printings. A "bible" among many in the counterculture of the 1960s, it is still in print today. Even with the book's critical failure though, right after its release in 1962 Aldous was made a Companion of Literature by the Royal Society of Literature in London. At the time there were only four previous recipients still alive: Winston Churchill, E.M. Forster, John Masefield, and Somerset Maugham. Aldous accepted the position as a great honor but was unable to attend the ceremony in London that summer because he had contracted cancer of the throat.

Two years earlier, in the spring of 1960, Aldous had had a previous bout of cancer, the illness that had cost him his mother and first wife. At that time it had appeared as a bump on his tongue that made eating painful. A biopsy had showed there was a malignancy and surgery had been advised, but Aldous and Laura had decided against having part of his tongue removed too quickly as Aldous was making the biggest part of his living as a lecturer. After a second medical opinion they had decided to have him treated with radium needles and outpatient radiation therapy, which, it seems, did cure the disease. However, in 1962 a new cancer developed and Aldous was now having pain in his jaw and neck.

His doctor, Max Cutler, who had treated him for the earlier cancer, examined Aldous and decided to remove a gland from the side of his neck. Surgery showed that the gland was infected and Cutler did what he could to remove the malignancy. That summer Aldous underwent a series of fatiguing radiation treatments, entering the hospital under the name "Matthew Leonard." Cutler tried to reassure him, explaining that cancers of this kind were not usually serious. Whether he was trying to spare Aldous worry or not isn't clear, but within months Aldous was again having trouble, and in May of 1963 he entered the Cedars of Lebanon Hospital for observation. More radiation followed in June and July. Huxley's condition was serious; however, by fall he was feeling a bit stronger and he was able to travel to Europe for one last visit.

He went to Stockholm, Sweden, for a meeting of the World Academy of Arts and Sciences, where he met with Humphry Osmond, the doctor who had first given him mescaline, for the last time. At the meeting they proposed that the Academy not only study "World Resources" but also "Human Resources," the yet untapped potentialities of spirit and mind that could help build a better world. The Academy agreed and charged Huxley and Osmond to outline those resources—a project Aldous would never complete. After Stockholm, Huxley went to England to visit friends and relatives and, though neither he nor they knew it at the time, to say good-bye. Unfortunately; he was unable to see Gervas Huxley, the cousin with whom he had been so close as a child. Gervas was sick, too, and Aldous wrote him to wish him well, remarking, "'Growing old gracefully'—it isn't easy when the physiological machine starts to break down.... One learns the Second Law of Thermodynamics by direct experience."

Returning to the United States at the end of August, Huxley was delighted to find that a book Laura had published in May, *You Are Not the Target*, was still selling very well. The book, based on her experiences as a therapist, had already sold more than 100,000 copies and would go on to sell over a quarter of a million. This buoyed Aldous's mood not only because it was a success for Laura but because the book was filled with "recipes" for consciousness-expansion and compassion-building that he believed would be useful to people. Huxley had in a sense already endorsed Laura's techniques in *Island* by incorporating several of them "almost unmodified, into my phantasy."

Laura had to travel that fall to promote her book and was often gone from home; however, she canceled several engagements when Aldous's health continued to weaken. He continued working on his projects but by late September he was writing to Julian about the seriousness of his condition. By mid-October his condition had become even worse and Laura notified Matthew, who immediately came to spend a few days with his father. During Matthew's visit Aldous perked up a bit, even getting out of bed for tea on Matthew's last day with him. Even at the end he remained lucid and engaged with life. Isherwood, who visited Aldous on November fifth later said, "I came away with the picture of a great noble vessel sinking quietly into the deep; many of its delicate marvelous mechanisms still in perfect order, all its lights still shining." Aldous was still working— and it is a testimony to his work ethic that he finished his last article, "Shakespeare and Religion," just two days before he died.

The lucidity of Huxley's mind in those last days is of particular significance, because on November 22, the day he died, he asked Laura to give him LSD. As Heard would later explain in his comments for the *Memorial Volume*, Aldous was not seeking to be medicated—and, in fact, had minimized his intake of opiates—but was formulating a last bold experiment. In a letter to Osmond in 1958 he had wondered if LSD were given to a terminal cancer patient would it "make dying a more spiritual, less strictly physiological process."

Now he was going to find out. He scribbled on a note to Laura, "Try LSD 100 mm intramuscular."

His doctor, Max Cutler, was already at their home, a new house on Mulholland Drive, along with Rosalind Rajagopal and other friends, and Laura conferred with him about Aldous's request. Cutler had some reservations but finally consented and Laura herself gave him the LSD injection—the first of two doses—around 11:45 a.m. "Then I began to talk to him," Laura later wrote, "saying 'light and free.'" It was Laura's intention to guide Aldous as he had once guided Maria. She talked to him periodically all afternoon, refraining, as he had requested, from asking questions and offering only encouragement. In her book she explains that the one question she asked was Can you hear me? and he confirmed that he could. She then continued:

> Light and free you let go, darling; forward and up.
> You are going forward and up; you are going toward
> the light. . . .You are doing it so beautifully, so easily.
> Light and free. Forward and up. You are going to-
> ward Maria's love with my love. You are going to-
> ward a greater love than you have ever known. You
> are going toward the best, the greatest love, and it is
> easy, it is so easy, and you are doing it so beautiful-
> ly.[4]

Aldous was in the full embrace of the LSD, an experiential truth he believed in—preferring to enter his death, spiritually speaking, with eyes wide open. He would die as he had lived—with courage and curiosity. And then finally, "the breathing became slower and slower, and there was absolutely not the slightest indication of contraction, of struggle . . and at five-twenty the breathing stopped."

Matthew arrived too late to say one last goodbye to his father. The airports and train stations had been in chaos that day because of the assassination of the U.S. president, John F. Kennedy, in Dallas, Texas. One testimony to Aldous's fame was that the constant news, on radio and TV, about Kennedy having been shot, was often interrupted to report that Huxley had also died. Huxley was cremated the next day without religious ceremony and that afternoon, at Matthew's suggestion, his relatives and close friends honored him by taking a walk along the route he himself took almost every afternoon. Stravinsky did not attend and was for some time inconsolable. For the *Memorial Volume* Stravinsky wrote a letter explaining that he had not only lost a friend but a spiritual guide. Later he composed a suite dedicated to Aldous Huxley. And so the author and visionary whom Thomas Mann had called "one of the finest flowerings of Western European intellectualism" was gone.

# - 12 -

## A MYSTICAL AGNOSTIC

*Doubt is an uncomfortable condition,*
*but certainty is a ridiculous one.*
—Voltaire

HUXLEY WAS A PHILOSOPHER but his viewpoint was not determined by the intellect alone. He believed the rational mind could
only speculate about truth and never find it directly. As he once put
it, "All too frequently Western philosophy, above all modern Western
philosophy, is pure speculation based on theoretical knowledge that
ends only in theoretical conclusions."

Huxley was most certainly a mystic, believing specifically that
there is an ultimate substrate of existence, Eckhart's "divine ground,"
which connects all things in a web of life and that can be known experientially—giving wisdom to the mind, love to the heart, and
meaning to one's life. Leonard Woolf once called Aldous the blind
seer "looking inward rather than outward for the truth and finding
it."

But exactly what kind of a mystic was Huxley? Gerald Heard,
who knew him well and was very familiar with mysticism, once speculated for the *Kenyon Review* in 1965 that Huxley's viewpoint was closest to that of Theravada Buddhism. Certainly it is easy to understand
why. Theravada Buddhists believe that the Buddha was only a man,
not a god or a godlike being, and that he is valuable to us only as a
role model. The Buddha was a person and he became enlightened,
therefore, all persons are capable of becoming enlightened.

Theravadins do not believe that we can grow spiritually except through our own efforts. No lord will bend down to lift us up. Huxley liked the worldliness of this viewpoint and the weight it placed on personal initiative. However, Huxley did not agree with the Theravadin emphasis on monasticism and strict meditation practices, and preferred the Mahayana Buddhist cultivation of compassion and social activism over the Theravadins' goal of personal realization. Huxley wrote, "The kingdom of God is within us but at the same time it is our business to contribute to the founding of the Kingdom of God upon earth."

We could not say, however, that Huxley was a Mahayana Buddhist—for several reasons, including that he did not agree with its belief in the efficacy of praying for grace to a variety of celestial Buddhas. The Hindu doctrine of Advaita Vedanta comes closest to Huxley's viewpoint, and it's significant that Aldous kept a connection with the Vedanta Society all his life—and with Krishnamurti, whose own system closely parallels Vedanta. But Huxley did not believe in doctrines and he firmly believed that no doctrine could be perfectly accurate to the experiential truth itself. Huxley's "perennial philosophy" is only a rational approximate of the truth, and so he held it provisionally rather than dogmatically. Ultimately, and especially with regards to intellectual knowledge, Huxley must be called an agnostic—true to the term his grandfather had first invented. He defined his position clearly in June of 1962, in a letter, "I remain an agnostic who aspires to be a Gnostic—but a gnostic only on the mystical level, a gnostic without symbols, cosmologies or a pantheon."[1]

Huxley wished to be both pragmatic and mystical—and he believed his viewpoint allowed for that. He interpreted the various descriptions of the "beatific vision" as analogues that could lead people to embrace the direct experience but warned that the descriptions must not be confused for enlightenment itself. Huxley sometimes referred to a Zen story about a monk who is walking on a mountain trail and who sees his teacher ahead of him pointing to the sky. When the monk follows his teacher's finger, he sees the moon rising over a pine bough and he becomes elated by its beauty. Huxley believed that intellectual analogues act like the Zen finger leading to transcendence, but that if they become enshrined as the truth itself, they create only idolatry and deception. One must embrace them provisionally and keep open to the fact that they are inferior to the "moon" itself.

In his preface to Krishnamurti's *The First and Last Freedom* he writes: "The man who has successfully solved the problem of his relations with the two worlds of data and symbols, is a man who has no beliefs. With regard to the problems of practical life he entertains a series of working hypotheses, which serve his purposes, but are taken no more seriously than any other kind of tool or instrument."

Because these working hypotheses are conceived of only as analogues one doesn't have to hold them in contradiction to scientific facts. "There is no conflict between the mystical approach to religion and the scientific approach, because one is not committed by mysticism to any cut-and-dried statement about the structure of the universe. You can practice mysticism entirely in psychological terms, and on the basis of a complete agnosticism in regard to the conceptual ideas of orthodox religion and yet come to knowledge—and the fruits of knowledge."[2]

Another characteristic of Huxley's mysticism is that it is, as Lawrence would have liked, very this-worldly. For Huxley, mysticism's rewards are enjoyed in the realm of everyday experience, and for many readers, this is the attraction to Huxley. He attempted to balance the transcendent with the mundane. As Huston Smith, an important authority on world religions, once remarked, "Huxley's regard for mysticism was well known by dint of being so nearly notorious. What some overlooked was equal interest in the workaday world. . . . To those who, greedy for transcendence, deprecated the mundane, he counseled that 'we must make the best of *both* worlds.' To their opposites, the positivists, his word was 'Alright, one world at a time; but not *half* a world.'"[3]

Huxley's highest truth—the enlightenment experience itself, as well as his interpretation of it—was also held provisionally. Even here Huxley was ultimately an agnostic, though one who "aspired" to be a gnostic. Without the experience of permanent enlightenment, an omega point in his experiment to prove its existence, he could only hold to this truth provisionally, as a best guess based upon compelling personal experiences, with and without psychedelics. And because Huxley never became fully a gnostic his journey never ended. He was, as went the motto of his school for children, "still learning." This is why—enlightenment never having been verified—he said at a public talk near the end of his life, "It is a little embarrassing that, after forty-five years of research and study, the best advice I can give to people is to be a little kinder to each other." This is also why his critics could never really pin him down. As Timothy Leary once observed, "The man just wouldn't stop and pose for the definitive portrait."

Many of those who came to hear Aldous Huxley's lectures at Berkeley, MIT and elsewhere found great meaning and purpose in his words. For them, he was a prophet and visionary. They trusted Huxley's integrity and believed, like Huxley himself, that we must avoid the idolatries of nationalism and materialism. They agreed with him that we must avoid vulgarity in our personal lives and mediocrity in our arts and education. That we must fight the centralization of power because of its tendencies toward war and erosion of personal freedom. That we must not let ourselves be driven by science and technology. That we must include the natural world and its many species in our calculations of progress. In this last regard, he stated, "The proper study of mankind is Man and, next to Man, mankind's properest study is Nature—that Nature of which he is an emergent part and with which, if he hopes to survive as a species, if he aspires to actualize the best of his individual and collective potentialities, he must learn to live in harmony. . . . Would we like to be well treated by Nature? Then we must treat Nature well. . . . For the ecologist, man's inhumanity to Nature deserves almost as strong a condemnation as man's inhumanity to man."

Huxley, standing tall at the podium, urged his audiences also to remember that the search for truth begins with an open mind. That truth should never be dogmatic and that by respecting the knowledge of others, we can keep opening out into the mystery of the world in a meaningful way. Keeping open will help us to realize the relativity of cultural values and also help us to bring the sciences and the humanities more closely together, watching out for the higher purposes of the human race. In the last paragraph of the last book Huxley published in his lifetime, *Literature and Science*, he summarizes his entire philosophy and offers this advice:

> Thought is crude, matter unimaginably subtle. Words are few and can only be arranged in certain conventionally fixed ways; the counterpoint of unique events is infinitely wide and their succession indefinitely long. That the purified language of science, or even the richer purified language of literature should ever be adequate to the givenness of the world and of our experience, is in the very nature of things, impossible. Cheerfully, accepting this fact, let us advance together, men of letters and men of science, further and further into the ever-expanding regions of the unknown.

# CHRONOLOGY

1894    Aldous Leonard Huxley is born at Godalming, Surrey, July 26. He is the third son, after Julian and Trevenen, of Leonard Huxley and Julia Arnold Huxley. Five years later, in 1899, his sister Margaret is born.

1901    Julia Huxley starts Prior's Field School.

1908    After five years of education at Hillside School, Aldous enters Eton in September. His mother, Julia, dies in November.

1909    Leonard Huxley moves to London to work in the publishing in dustry. The Huxley children spend most holidays with relatives— Aldous usually with his aunt, the novelist, Mrs. Humphry Ward.

1910    Aldous leaves Eton after suffering a severe inflammation of the eyes. Learns Braille and continues to educate himself.

1913    Enters Balliol at Oxford with the support and coaching of his brother, Trevenen.

1914    In August Trevenen commits suicide. Aldous returns to Oxford in October, resides with the Haldane family.

1915    First visit to Garsington Manor, the home of Philip and Ottoline Morrell. First meetings with Maria Nys (his future wife), D.H, Lawrence, and Virginia Woolf.

1916    Publishes his first book of poetry, *The Burning Wheel*, in September. Graduates from Oxford with a First in English literature. Begins an eight month stay at Garsington. Establishes friendships with John Middleton Murray, Katherine Mansfield, and Bertrund Russell, and is courting Maria Nys.

1919    Moves to London, joins the editorial staff of the *Atheneum* under Middleton Murray. Develops closer friendship with TS. Eliot, whom he had first met at Garsington. Married, July 10, to Maria Nys.

1919    Matthew Huxley, only child of Aldous and Maria, born on April 19.

1920    Vacations for the summer in Italy, at Forte dei Marmi. Writes his first novel, *Crome Yellow*, based on his time at Garsington.

| | |
|---|---|
| **1925** | After publishing two more novels, Aldous takes a round-the-world trip, described in *Jesting Pilate*. |
| **1926** | Aldous and Maria begin a close friendship with D.H. Lawrence and his wife, Frieda. |
| **1928** | The Huxleys, including Julian and his wife, Juliette, vacation at Les Diablerets, Switzerland with Lawrence and Frieda. Maria Huxley types manuscript of *Lady Chatterley's Lover*. Aldous works mornings on *Point Counter Point*. |
| **1930** | Death of D.H. Lawrence in March. Huxleys move to Sanary, France, in April. |
| **1933** | A few months after the publication of *Brave New World*, Huxleys travel to West Indies, Central America, Mexico, and the United States. Death of Leonard Huxley in May. |
| **1934** | Huxleys winter in London. Aldous has insomnia and is having trouble writing. Friendship with Gerald Heard, whom he first met in 1929, is deepening. |
| **1934** | Becomes active, along with Heard, in the pacifist movement. |
| **1937** | Aldous, Maria, and Heard sail for the United States aboard the *S.S. Normandie*. Visit Frieda Lawrence in New Mexico. Aldous writes *Ends and .Means*. Huxleys visit Hollywood and first meet Edwin Hubble, Charlie Chaplin, and Paulette Goddard. |
| **1939** | Aldous works on script for *Pride and Prejudice* for MGM, studies with Swami Prabhavananda and begins his friendship with Christopher Isherwood. |
| **1942** | Huxleys move to the desert at Llano, California. Aldous writes *The Art of Seeing* and learns to drive a car. Explores meditation practices suggested by his friend Krishnamurti. |
| **1945** | Aldous publishes *The Perennial Philosophy* and writes *Science, Liberty, and Peace*. |
| **1942** | Huxleys have moved back into Los Angeles. Matthew Huxley, after graduation from Berkeley, marries Ellen Hovde. Aldous publishes Themes and Variations. |
| **1951** | Severe attack of iritis affects Aldous's right eye. Matthew and Ellen have a son, Mark Trevenen Huxley-. |
| **1952** | Aldous publishes *The Devils of Loudun*. Maria is operated on for breast cancer; the disease recurs after six months. |
| **1953** | Aldous first takes mescaline, under the supervision of Dr. Humphry Osmond. |
| **1955** | Huxley contracts to write articles regularly for *Esquire*. Death of |

Maria Huxley in February. Aldous summers in Connecticut with Matthew, Ellen, and their children, Mark and Tessa (born in October, 1953).

**1956** Publishes *Heaven and Hell* and *Adonis and the Alphabet*. Marries Laura Archera at the drive-in wedding chapel in Yuma, Arizona, March 19.

**1959** Huxley is a visiting professor at the University of California at Santa Barbara, receives his first honorary doctoral degree, and is awarded the Award of Merit Medal by the American Academy of Arts and Letters.

**1960** Visiting professorships at the Menninger Foundation, Topeka, and the Massachusetts Institute of Technology, Cambridge. First meeting with Timothy Leary. Huxley is diagnosed with cancer of the tongue.

**1961** His house in the hills above Los Angeles is consumed by fire, destroying his library.

**1962** Visiting professor at Berkeley. Publishes his last novel, *Island*, and is designated a Campanion of Literature. In July he undergoes surgery to remove a neck gland that is found to contain malignancy.

**1963** Attends meeting of the World Academy of Arts and Sciences in Stockholm. Last visit to England and Italy. Composes "Shakespeare and Religion" on his deathbed. Dies on November 22. His body is cremated the same day.

# NOTES

CHAPTER 1: A NEW REFORMATION
1. Ronald Clark, *The Huxleys*.
2. Quoted in William Irvine, *Apes, Angels, and Victorians*, p.198.
3. Joseph Wood, Krutch, *The Modern Temper*, p.53.

CHAPTER 2: THREE CRISES
1. Quoted in Ronald Clark, *The Huxleys*, p.148.
2. Matthew Arnold, *Culture and Anarchy*.
3. Aldous Huxley, *The Art of Seeing*.
4. Sybille Bedford, *Aldous Huxley, A Biography*, pp.44-45.
5. Grover Smith, ed., *Letters of Aldous Huxley*, p.61.

CHAPTER 3: GARSINGTON
1. Grover Smith, ed., *The Letters of Aldous Huxley*, p.63.
2. Alexander Henderson, *Aldous Huxley*, p.12.
3. Cyril Connolly, *Enemies of Promise*, p.52.
4. Leonard Woolf in Julian Huxley, ed., *Aldous Huxley, A Memorial Volume*, p.34.
5. Smith, p.143.
6. Sybille Bedford, *Aldous Huxley, A Biography*, p.121.
7. Jocelyn Brooke, *Aldous Huxley*, 1954.
8. Kenneth Clark in Julian Huxley, ed., *Aldous Huxley, A Memorial Volume*, p.17.
9. John Strachey, quoted in Ronald Clark, *The Huxleys*, p.214.
10. David Bowering, *Aldous Huxley, A Study of the Major Novels*, p.21.
11. Ronald Clark, p.218.
12. Aldous Huxley, *The Olive Tree*, p.43.
13. Huxley, *Jesting Pilate*, p.325.

CHAPTER 4: D.H. LAWRENCE
1. Nicolson and Trautmann, eds., *Letters of Virginia Woolf* Vol. IV, p.293.
2. Grover Smith, ed., *The Letters of Aldous Huxley*, p.242.
3. Milton Birnbaum, *Aldous Huxley's Quest for Values*, p.70.
4. Aldous Huxley, ed., *The Letters of D.H. Lawrence*, p.96.

5. Ibid., p.xviii.
6. Quoted in Sybille Bedford, *Aldous Huxley, A Biography*, p.192.
7. Smith, p.314.
8. Ibid., p.332.
9. Quoted in Alexander Henderson, *Aldous Huxley*, p.39.

CHAPTER 5: BRAVE NEW WORLD

1. Quoted in Hermione Lee, *Virginia Woolf* p.530.
2. Anthony Burgess, *The Novel Today*, 1963.
3. Aldous Huxley, *The Olive Tree*, pp.41-42.
4. Matthew Arnold, *The Works of Matthew Arnold*, Vol. VI, p.47.
5. Julian Huxley, ed., *Aldous Huxley, A Memorial Volume*, p.100.
6. Aldous Huxley, "The Victory of Art over Humanity," in David Brad shaw, ed., *Aldous Huxley Between the Wars*.
7. Huxley, in "Spinoza's Worm," *Do What You Will*, p. 71.
8. Huxley, "The Outlook for American Culture: Some Reflections in the Machine Age," in *Proper Studies*.
9. Robert S. Baker, *The Dark Historic Page*, p.139.
10. J.F.C. Fuller quoted in Peter Edgerly Firchow; *The End of Utopia: A Study of Aldous Huxley's Brave New World*, p.103.
11. For example, see Firchow, p.33.
12. Grover Smith, *The Letters of Aldous Huxley*, p.2.
13. Quoted in Alexander Henderson, Aldous Huxley, p.171. See also Hux ley's essay, "Tragedy and the Whole Truth," from *Music at Night* for more of this view.

CHAPTER 6: COMING TO AMERICA

1. Aldous Huxley, *Ends and Means*, p.11.
2. Sybille Bedford, *Aldous Huxley, A Biography*, p.324.
3. John V Cody, "Gerald Heard, Soul Guide to the Beyond Within," *Gnosis*, no.26, p.64.
4. Gerald Heard, *The Third Morality*, p.157.
5. Huxley, *Eyeless in Gaza*, p.343.
6. Grover Smith, ed., *The Letters of Aldous Huxley*, p.382.
7. Huxley, *The Perennial Philosophy*, p.14.
8. Huxley, *Eyeless in Gaza*, p.372.
9. Ibid., p.471-472.
10. Huxley, *Ends and Means*, p.309-310.
11. David King Dunaway, *Huxley in Hollywood*, p.78.

CHAPTER 7: THE PERENNIAL PHILOSOPHY
1. Grover Smith, ed., *The Letters of Aldous Huxley*, p.428.
2. Troy Wilson Organ, *Hinduism: Its Historical Development*, p.57.
3. John Lehmann, *Christopher Isherwood, A Personal Memoir*, p.53.
4. Most prominently, in Christopher Isherwood, ed., *Vedanta for Modern Man* and *Vedanta for the Western World*.
5. Aldous Huxley, *Ends and Means*, in chapt. 13, "Religious Practices," p. 272.
6. Quoted in Mary Lutyens, Krishnamurti: *The Years of Fulfillment*, p.45.
7. Ibid., p.7.
8. Ibid., p.58-59.
9. Quoted in Alan Watts, *In My Own Way*, p.118.
10. Lutyens, p.59. Compare also his discussion of meditation on p.172.
11. Ronald Clark, *The Huxleys*, p.295.
12. Quoted in Sybille Bedford, Aldous Huxley, A Biography, p.435.
13. Christopher Isherwood in Julian Huxley, ed., Aldous Huxley, A Memorial Volume, p.158.
14. Bedford, p.438: "Aldous insisted on the insertion of this line, `Mr. Huxley has made no attempts to found a new religion'. And in Smith, Letters, p.525 Aldous tells his editor that this line should "take the wind out of the sails of some of the ecclesiastical critics who will want to say that I am another Mrs. Eddy," referring to the founder of The Church of Christ Scientist.

CHAPTER 8:SCIENCE, LIBERTY, AND PEACE
1. Quoted in Ronald Clark, *The Huxleys*, p.303. See also information in David King Dunaway, *Huxley in Hollywood*, no. 108, pp.415-416.
2. Aldous Huxley, *Time Must Have a Stop*, p.146.
3. Ibid., p.3.
4. Valclav Havel (1936— ), Czech playwrite and author, who was imprisoned for several years and whose books were banned during the Soviet period. In 1989 he was elected president of the liberated Czechoslovakia.
5. Aldous Huxley, *Themes and Variations*, p.43.
6. Huxley, *Science, Liberty, and Peace*, p.32.
7. Huxley, *Themes and Variations*, p.241.
8. Ibid., p.272.
9. June Decry, *Aldous Huxley and the Mysticism of Science*, p.171.
10. Huxley, *Themes and Variations*, p.84.

11. Grover Smith, ed., *The Letters of Aldous Huxley*, p.550.
12. Quoted in Sybille Bedford, *Aldous Huxley, A Biography*, p.503.
13. Dunaway, pp.225-226.
14. Ibid., p.253.

CHAPTER 9: THE DOORS OF PERCEPTION
1. Anita Loos in Julian Huxley, ed., *Aldous Huxley, A Memorial Volume*, p.95.
2. Aldous Huxley, *The Doors of Perception*, p.75.
3. Quoted in Sybille Bedford, *Aldous Huxley, A Biography*, p.518.
4. David King Dunaway, *Huxley in Hollywood*, p.265.
5. Bedford, p.552.
6. Humphry Osmond in Julian Huxley, ed., *Aldous Huxley, A Memorial Volume*, p.118.
7. Quoted in Masters and Houston, *The Varieties of Psychedelic Experience*, p.47.
8. William James, *The Varieties of Religious Experience*, p.298.
9. Quoted in Ronald Clark, *The Huxleys*, p.348.
10. Huxley, *The Doors of Perception*, p.12.
11. Ibid., pp.22-23.
12. Ibid., p.36.
13. Ibid., p.19.
14. Aldous Huxley, *Island,* pp.271-272.
15. Huxley, *The Doors of Perception*, p.42.
16. Ibid., p.73.
17. Bedford, p.544.
18. Aldous Huxley, *Heaven and Hell*, p.63.
19. *Bhagavad—Gita,* II.46.
20. Grover Smith, ed., *The Letters of Aldous Huxley,* pp.735-737.

CHAPTER 10: DRIVE-IN WEDDING CHAPEL
1. Grover Smith, ed., *The Letters of Aldous Huxley*, p.740.
2. Laura Archera Huxley, *This Timeless Moment*, p.31.
3. From an interview, in David King Dunaway, *Huxley in Hollywood,* p.347.
4. Ronald Clark, *The Huxleys,* p.353.
5. Smith, p.870.
6. Ibid., p.801.
7. Ibid., p.704.
8. Quoted in Timothy Leary, *Flashbacks*, p.132.
9. Dunaway, p.327.

CHAPTER 11 : TIMOTHY LEARY

1.  Grover Smith, ed., *The Letters of Aldous Huxley*, p.945.
2.  Oliver Hockenhill, Aldous Huxley: The Gravity of Light (a Canadian film), 1996.
3.  Albert Hoffman, *LSD, My Problem Child*, chapt. 8, "Meeting with Aldous Huxley."
4.  Laura Huxley, *This Timeless Moment*, p.286.

CHAPTER 12: A MYSTICAL AGNOSTIC

1.  Grover Smith, ed., *The Letters of Aldous Huxley*, p.935.
2.  Aldous Huxley, *The Human Situation*, p.215.
3.  Huston Smith, *The Psychedelic Review*, Vol. 1, no.3, 1964.

# BOOKS BY HUXLEY

## NOVELS

*Crome Yellow* (1921)
*Antic Hay* (1923)
*Those Barren Leaves* (1925)
*Point Counter Point* (1928)
*Brave New World* (1932)
*Eyeless in Gaza* (1936)
*After Many a Summer Dies the Swan* (1939)
*Time Must Have a Stop* (1944)
*Ape and Essence* (1948)
*The Genius and the Goddess* (1955)
*Island* (1962)

## BOOKS OF ESSAYS

*On the Margin* (1923)
*Along the Road* (1925)
*Essays New and Old* (1926)
*Proper Studies* (1927)
*Do What You Will* (1929)
*Vulgarity in Literature* (1930)
*Music at Night* (1931)
*Texts and Pretexts* (1932)
*The Olive Tree* (1936)
*Ends and Means* (1937)
*The Art of Seeing* (1942)
*The Perennial Philosophy* (1945)
*Science, Liberty, and Peace* (1946)
*Themes and Variations* (1950)
*The Doors of Perception* (1954)
*Heaven and Hell* (1956)
*Adonis and the Alphabet* (1956)
*Collected Essays* (1958)

*Brave New World Revisited* (1958)
*Literature and Science* (1963)
*The Human Situation* (published posthumously, 1977)

## BOOKS OF SHORT STORIES

*Limbo* (1920)
*Mortal Coils* (1922)
*Little Mexican* (1924)
*Two or Three Graces* (1926)
*Brief Candles* (1930)
*Collected Short Stories* (1957)

## BIOGRAPHY

*Grey Eminence* (1941)
*The Devils of Loudun* (1952)

## POETRY

*The Burning Wheel* (1916)
*The Defeat of Youth* (1918)
*Leda* (1920)
*The Cicadas* (1931)

## TRAVEL

*Jesting Pilate* (1926)
*Beyond the Mexique Bay* (1934)

## DRAMA

*The World of Light* (1931)

# SELECTED BIBLIOGRAPHY

Arnold, Matthew. *Culture and Anarchy*, in *The Works of- Matthew Arnold*, Vol. VI, London: Macmillan, 1903.

Baker, Robert S. *Brave New World: History, Science, and Dystopia*, Boston: Twayne Publishers, 1990.

_____. *The Dark Historic Page: Social Satire and Historicism in the Novels of Aldous Huxley*, Madison: University of Wisconsin Press, 1982.

Bedford, Sybille. *Aldous Huxley, A Biography*, New York: Harper & Row, 1974.

Birnbaum, Milton. *Aldous Huxley's Quest for- Values*, Knoxville: University of Tennessee Press, 1971.

Bowering, David. *Aldous Huxley, A Study of the Major Novels*, New York: Oxford Press, 1969.

Bradshaw, David, ed. *Between the Wars: Essays and Letters of Aldous Huxley*, Chicago: I.R. Dee, 1994.

Brooke, Jocelyn. *Aldous Huxley*, London: Published for the British Council by Longmans, Green, 1954.

Burgess, Anthony. *The Novel Today*, London: Folcroft, 1963.

Clark, Ronald. *The Huxleys*, New York: McGraw-Hill, 1968.

Cody, John V "Gerald Heard, Soul Guide to the Beyond Within," *Gnosis*, no.26, 1993, pp.64-70.

Connolly, Cyril. *Enemies of Promise*, London: Routledge & Kegan Paul, 1938.

Decry, Jane. *Aldous Huxley and the Mysticism of Science*, New York: St. Martin's Press, 1996.

Dunaway, David King. *Huxley in Hollywood*, New York: Harper & Row, 1989.

Eiseley, Loren. *Darwin's Century*, Garden City, NY: Doubleday, 1961

Firchow, Peter Edgerly. *The End of Utopia: A Study of Aldous Huxley's Brave New World*, Lewisburg, PA: Bucknell University Press, 1984.

Gambhirananda, Swami. *History of Ramakrishna Math and Mission*, Calcutta: Advaita Ashrama, 1983.

Heard, Gerald. *The Eternal Gospel*, New York: Harper & Brothers, 1946.

_____. *The Third Morality*, New York: Morrow, 1937.

_____. "The Poignant Prophet" (a reflection on Aldous Huxley), *The Kenyon Review*, Nov. 1965, pp.49-70.

Henderson, Alexander. *Aldous Huxley*, New York: Harper & Brothers, 1936.

Holmes, Charles Mason. *Aldous Huxley and the Way to Reality*, Bloomington: Indiana University Press, 1970.

Huxley, Aldous, ed. *The Letters of D.H. Lawrence,* New York: The Viking Press, 1932.

Huxley, Julian, ed. *Aldous Huxley, A Memorial Volume*, New York: Harper & Row, 1965.

___. *Memories*, Vol. I, New York: Allen & Unwin, 1970.

Huxley, Laura Archera. *This Timeless Moment: A Personal View of Aldous Huxley*, New York: Farrar, Straus & Giroux, 1968.

___. *You Are Not the Target*, forward by Aldous Huxley, Hollywood, CA: Wilshire Books, 1963.

Irvine, William. *Apes, Angels, and Victorians,* Cleveland, Ohio: Meridian Books, 1955.

Isherwood, Christopher, ed. *Vedanta for Modern Man,* New York: Harper, 1951.

___. ed. *Vedanta for the Western World*, London: Allen & Unwin, 1948.

James, William. *The Varieties of Religious Experience*, New York: Mentor Books, 1958.

Krishnamurti, J. *The First and Last Freedom,* with an introduction by Aldous Huxley, Wheaton, IL: Theosophical Publishing House; 1954.

Krutch, Joseph Wood. *The Modern Temper,* New York: Harvest Books, 1956.

Lawrence, D.H. *Psychoanalysis and the Unconscious, Fantasia of the Unconscious,* New York: Viking Press, 1960.

Leary, Timothy. *Flashbacks*, New York: G.P. Putnam's Sons, 1990.

___. "Homage to Huxley," in *The Politics of Ecstasy*, New York: G.P. Putnam, 1968.

Lee, Hermione. *Virginia Woolf,* New York: Alfred A. Knopf, 1997.

Lehmann, John. *Christopher Isherwood: A Personal Memoir*, New York: Henry Holt, 1987.

Lutgens, Mary. *Krishnamurti: The Years of Fulfillment*, New York: Farrar, Straus, Giroux, 1983.

Masters, R.E.L. and Houston, Jean. *The Varieties of Psychedelic Experience*, New York: Delta Books, 1966.

Nicolson, Nigel and Tautmann, Joanne. *Letters of Virginia Woolf* Vol. VI, New York: Harcourt Brace Jovanovich, 1978.

Organ, Troy Wilson. *Hinduism: Its Historical Development*, Woodbury, NY: Barron's, 1974.

Smith, Grover, ed. *Letters of. Aldous Huxley*, New York: Harper & Row, 1969.

Thody, Philip. *Aldous Huxley, A Biographical Introduction,* New York: Charles Scribner's Sons, 1973.

Trilling, Lionel. *Matthew Arnold,* New York: Columbia University Press, 1949.

Watt, Donald. *Aldous Huxley, the Critical Heritage,* London: Routledge & Kagan Paul, 1975.

Watts, Alan W *In My Own Way,* New York: Pantheon Books, 1972.

____. The Joyous Cosmology, New -York.: Vintage Books, 1962.

Zaehner, R.C. *Zen, Drugs and Mysticism,* New York: Vintage Books, 1972.

# INDEX

Made in the USA
Lexington, KY
27 February 2017